LOOK AT THE COLORS TO THE LEFT...

Which one do you identify with most strongly—which one is "you"?

Which colors make you feel calm...secure...romantic ...excited?

Which colors leave you indifferent?

Which one is your "yuk" color—the color you dislike the most?

Discover the hidden secrets of colors—how they can help you solve daily problems and project a happy, healthy, and confident image.

THE LANGUAGE OF COLOR

THE
LANGUAGE
OF
COLOR

Dorothee L. Mella

WARNER BOOKS

A Time Warner Company

SICA copyright © 1972 Dorothee L. Mella #A494433
SICA Computer Program © added to copyright 1979 Dorothee L. Mella #A494433
SICA Systems Publication—revised copyright © 1985 #A494433
computer program—Savvy Data Base System—© 1984 Excalibur Technologies Corp

Copyright © 1988 by Dorothee L. Mella
All rights reserved.
Warner Books, Inc., 1271 Avenue of the Americas, New York, NY 10020

 A Time Warner Company
Printed in the United States of America
First Printing: September 1988
10 9 8 7 6 5 4

Book design by Giorgetta Bell McRee
Cover design by Suzanne Noli

Line illustrations by Mike Kimball
Color wheel photo by Phyllis Peck
Chart lay-outs by Printing Services

Library of Congress Cataloging-in-Publication Data

Mella, Dorothee L.
    The language of color / Dorothee L. Mella.
        p.   cm.
    Bibliography: p.

    1. Color—Psychological aspects.   2. Self-evaluation.   3. Self-
actualization (Psychology)   4. Environmental psychology.
I. Title.
BF789.C7M43 1988
155.9′ 1145—dc19   88-5684
ISBN 0-446-38781-9 (U.S.A.)   CIP

Contents

Many thanks to everyone who helped with, gave of their talents, and experienced the SICA, the grammar of color.

SPECIAL THANKS

TO all of the art students who created the beginnings of the language of color.

TO Emily, Jan and Loretta, my first co-partners and associates in Domel Color Communications.

TO Charlie and Michelle, my caring family.

TO Betty, Irene, Judith and Frances, work-mates and contributors to the SICA data base in Albuquerque, New Mexico.

TO the computer program designers, especially, Bob Pinto.

TO Karen, Louise and Jeanne for their consulting advice on the SICA book.

TO Leslie Keenan for her expert editing.

And a special thanks to Ramona, my associate and friend.

TO EACH OF YOU, I DEDICATE THIS BOOK.

Ode to Color

Colors are electrons

Visible, they occupy one octave of the
electromagnetic spectrum

To reach you, their rainbow vibrations move
at the speed of light

Yet, they require no medium
for transmission

Learn from your colors, for they are part of you:
mind, eye, and sensation

Use your colors, for they are your personal resource
from the universe

—Dorothee L. Mella

Introduction
to the Self-image
Color Analysis (SICA)

Color had always been important to me as an artist. But my real interest in color psychology began in the late 1960s while I was teaching painting at the Maryland School of Art and Design. I was having a particularly difficult time with an advanced painting class because of the unalloyed mix of students, serious artists, hippies, housewives, and three retired military colonels.

It was obvious that there would be a communication problem from the first day I walked into the classroom. There was no interaction among the students. After looking each other over, they were safely entrenched in opposing corners. "I will listen to you, teacher, if that guy over there will take a bath once a week," one colonel remarked, typifying the attitudes of the group.

In the midst of my frustration I happened upon a journal kept by the famous abstract artist Wassily Kandinsky. Among his writings, in *The Art of Spiritual Harmony*, I found a poignant statement: "Color acts upon the human body; it is the key touched by man to obtain the appropriate vibration from his creative spirit." These words inspired me to conduct an experi-

1

ment with this noncommunicative class, using color as the main medium.

With renewed zeal I asked the class to paint a walk in the woods as an introspective exploration using only color—no representational form. "Identify your woods with a color. Make four other colors to harmonize and four more to contrast," I told them. "Don't use trees, rocks, or even mountains, use only your colors." They began their task with excited concentration, oblivious of their classmates for the first time.

When the hour for the final critique of the day arrived, the paintings were placed around the room for all to see. A hush enveloped everyone, except for the same colonel, who broke the silence. "Hippie, you've been in my woods! Your painting looks exactly like mine! You can't be so bad if you feel the woods as I do."

I realized there must be some truth to Kandinsky's ideas: color choice did express an individual's inner feelings. My students' sudden talking and laughing stimulated my determination to continue the color experimentation.

And I had willing helpers. All the students were excited about what their studies revealed about themselves. We worked with more abstractions. Then we began to develop a color language that eventually revealed how persons can identify, through individual color choice, their inner feelings.

The first SICA (Self-image Color Analysis) was a compilation of forty questions expressing an individual's self-portrait. Questions such as "What color represents me?" and "What color makes me feel warm, cold, fatigued, happy, sad, etc.?" were correlated for similarities and differences. As eight hundred SICAs were tallied by the art students from among family and friends, the beginnings of a language of color emerged. Not surprisingly, artists, their families, and their friends readily chose colors to express their moods, desires, and feelings. Others from outside the art profession were more reluctant to express themselves in color. However, some amazing similarities were discovered among the outsiders. Extroverts and those in expressive professions such as sales selected bright identity colors: reds, oranges, and yellows. Those who relied more upon intuitive and thoughtful abilities in their jobs chose cooler pastel colors for their self-portraits. The color test and increased self-awareness were put to use in helping students motivate desired change.

How strong an influence color produced in my life! I searched for credible verification of my findings on the individualized color responses and color identities in reference library books, but I found little to substantiate the color interpretations. My peers in the art society were supportive of what I had stumbled upon, but could not aid in documenting my work.

Then one of my favorite art students, a psychiatrist who was exploring alternative methods of diagnosing his drug-addicted patients, introduced me to *The Luscher Color Test* by Dr. Max Luscher. It was then used by physicians only. I was extremely impressed with his color test once it had been demonstrated, as I was the one who was examined. My only objection was not directed toward the color psychology test itself. I felt that there should also be available to the general public a simplified self-portrait method—one where individuals would have the opportunity to choose their *own personal palette* of colors to express their feelings about themselves. And why not an easy coloring system making everyone an artist, in order to portray the average woman and man of society who were wanting only to visualize their positive image and strengths for better communication purposes? Mainly for this reason, I decided to continue on the course of color study that I had set for myself, that of discovery of a language of color. (If you're interested in a color test that gives a scientific and psychological insight into your personality, Dr. Luscher's book is still widely available in paperback form today.) Color had a powerful effect on the life of my psychiatrist friend also, as he was in time to help begin one of the first art therapy departments at a major university in the Washington, D.C., area, which was to explore and teach diverse art forms for self-help.

Rumors about my color work brought new associates into my life, either to participate in collecting more SICA data, or to inquire if the results of the SICA could solve color design or color environmental problems. In response to this interest in color awareness, I formed a consulting company in 1971 with two copartners, a sociologist and a design communications specialist. We began consulting and problem-solving in business and government. We offered workshops on color self-profiling and personal design, and we gave the SICA a new format. We consolidated the number of questions, but the principal ones remained the same ("What color represents you?" or "If you could be a color, what color would you choose to identify yourself as?" etc.). Those who participated in the many color-painting workshops added more input to the expanding SICA data, since they came from all walks of life—lawyers and government employees alike.

Throughout the years—in tandem with my roles of artist, color analyst, and color communications consultant—I have personally served in the administration of over thirty thousand SICAs. My associates have tirelessly gathered information on the beneficial effects resulting from individual and corporate use of the SICA, both for image enhancement and for colors for environmental support. The computerization of the language of color, involving many hours of integration and analysis and many more hours of data processing, has enabled us to discover tally-composite color profiles of many different professional and working peoples. These portraits have given insight into group color choices, group color identities, and group "yuk" color dislikes—information used for design and image problem-solving needs. Out data excluded economic, racial, and religious information, for we sought only information pertinent to individual preference of color; and mainly, how one would identify through SICA with oneself.

Now that the color language has been put on computer, this twenty-year-old art language has been experienced by thousands of people, the meek and powerful alike. The positive results continue to amaze me as I receive letter after letter of thanks attesting to its success.

I have written this book in response to the request of many people who want to analyze their own color portrait. I feel that SICA can be a tremendous help to individuals, enabling them to know themselves better—an open door to inner communication. We all have the potential to be what we want to be, and often we just require the right tool to help us find the way. Each one of us is an artist in our own special right, creating and communicating ourselves every day. In a world so full of messages and media persuasions, each of us needs a strong sense of our own identity and self-worth. Often our overstimulating environment prevents us from being able to recognize our own special talent or potential. By achieving this self-recognition we grow in self-acceptance and become more creative in our lives—true contributors to society.

I hope that like thousands of others before you who have experienced the SICA, you will have fun playing with your colors. Take the knowledge and create more power in your life!

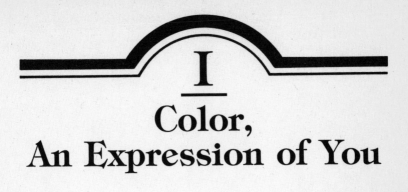

I

Color,
An Expression of You

1

The Fascination
of Color

The effects of color on our minds and bodies is a subject of increasing interest. Scientific studies show that red raises the blood pressure, quickens the pulse, and increases the rate of breathing. Blue, by contrast, slows down body activity and stimulates the mind. These facts, along with other scientific and empirical evidence, are already widely used by the fashion and advertising industries for profit. Ever notice the popular fast-food chains have high-energy colors such as orange in their interiors? Orange is not only a strong appetite stimulant, but it can make the viewer impatient and restless, encouraging the patrons to "eat and run." Men always remember the "woman in red" because that hue is the strongest and longest ray in the visible spectrum, making a greater impression on the retina, not to mention speeding up the emotions! Green, in the middle of the spectrum, has a calming, balancing effect. It can even reduce eyestrain, especially in a minty shade such as the one chosen by hospitals in their operating and recovery rooms. Have you ever noticed a yellow flyer in your advertising papers and junk mail? This stimulating color was used on purpose to make eye contact—

yours—to promote upcoming sales. In many modern office and professional decors there's a popular surge of mauves and violets. Is it a fad, or a revolution—a reaction to the increasing number of sensitive women in the work force? Violets and purples in the sixties were identified with a spiritual-awakening movement. Now, in the eighties, the prevalent use of mauve may reflect a true picture of the intuitive in the workplace. Multiple uses for the psychological uses of color are becoming more common each day. All are stimulating you, the public, to become more aware of the strong influence of color energy.

What is color and why is it important? This fascinating question continues to intrigue us. Color is reflected light. We feel it and see it through our eyes, our sensory makeup, and our minds. Humans can see 40 percent of the rays of light energy as the visible spectrum, the rainbow of color. (Many people believe that our sensitivity to color perception is on the increase as we're listening more and more to our feelings. Tomorrow we may see and perceive colors yet to be recognized by our eyes today.) These vibrations of electromagnetic energy travel from the sun to reach us. Upon contact, they penetrate our bodies through our eyes and skin—sending instant signals to our brain. When we lie out-of-doors in the sun our bodies absorb light energy. That same energy in a lesser intensity is color. Colors stimulate an emotional and mental response to what our eyes and bodies record. Strong energy is present in all bright, warm colors, as they are the longest rays of the visible spectrum of light. Not so with the cooler blues and violets or pastel colors, whose intensities are lesser in length and strength. Our brains, the masters of our bodies, respond to each vibratory electron of color, accepting or rejecting each sensation. Color, then, is a sensation of light. Color is a resource of passive solar energy!

Throughout the ages a number of master scientists have attempted to explain the principles of color and light. Sir Isaac Newton, in the seventeenth century, discovered the visible spectrum and mapped how light breaks into wavelengths of radiant energy. By producing the first indoor rainbow while directing a beam of light through a prism, he gave science its first major clue in its investigation of the universe. (Duplicating Newton's prism, the modern spectroscope detects the very nature of matter. No other device has performed as accurately in determining the formation of our galaxy.) In his renowned book *Opticks*, Newton arranged his hues to form the original color wheel, explaining the phenomena of diffraction and interference, or the bending of light. This revealing discovery proved to be the foundation of the science of the physics of light. Where colors were previously used to symbolize the mysteries of the universe, their function could now become the means of revealing them.

The most famous of all modern physicists, Dr. Albert Einstein, advanced our space-age awareness with the knowledge and understanding of the complete spectrum of electromagnetic energy—that is, light—how its energy travels through the universe. Without Einstein's genius, measurements of the speed of light and understandings of wavelengths would not have taken place. Our universe can now be explored and realized more fully because of his efforts. Telephones, radios, satellites, X rays, computers, gamma rays, and cosmic rays, as well as color, have all become a common part of our lives.

Artists, musicians, and philosophers, such as Da Vinci, Kandinsky, Goethe, Scriabin, Steiner, and Rimsky-Korsakov, have developed theories about the relationship between color, music, and the inner self. In *The Rainbow Book*, edited by F. Lanier Graham, one can read many connective essays on the ancient and modern physics of the spectrum—light, color, music, and the stars. One theme flows throughout all hypotheses. Color is to sight as sound is to hearing; both are vibrational movements of the universe. As energy waves, both are capable of reflection, diffraction, refraction, and interference. Their physical phenomena of intensity, frequency, and wave form create in us our perception of loudness, pitch, and tone in music; and in color, our awareness to intensity, hue, and shade.

LIGHT SPECTRUM

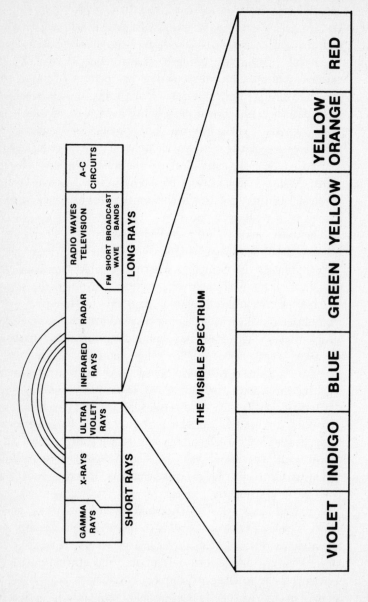

GAMMA RAYS	X-RAYS	ULTRA VIOLET RAYS	INFRARED RAYS	RADAR	RADIO WAVES TELEVISION	A-C CIRCUITS

FM SHORT WAVE BROADCAST BANDS

SHORT RAYS

LONG RAYS

THE VISIBLE SPECTRUM

VIOLET	INDIGO	BLUE	GREEN	YELLOW	YELLOW ORANGE	RED

Color has always been honored with symbolic designations in various cultures through time. We know through hieroglyphic records that the Egyptians placed value on the sun colors. Because of archaeological finds in various parts of the world, we have discovered ancient mystical identities for colors. They represented day, night, birth, life, death, water, and much, much more. Although limited in shades and hues, colors were also favored to signify man himself; his relationship to his gods, his spirit, his body, his earth, and his actions. An ancient Egyptian papyrus even depicts a healing treatment that prescribed the color red. In China, the emperor reserved the color gold for his personal use. The Romans experimented with the "Pompeii reds"; the Greeks lavished their robes and designs with emerald greens and peacock blues. Was it because the Greeks lived by the sea that they were influenced by oceanic colors; the Romans focused on delight and physical satisfaction, thus the color red; and the rulers of China desired magnificence, as gold expressed power?

To explore all the historical mysteries of color of each civilization would fill a book in itself. Color is one of the most intriguing topics of yesterday. As a subject, it offers investigation into almost every field of study, from mythology, anthropology, and architecture to science, medicine, and psychology. All yield vast sources of information concerning color uses, sometimes unexplained but always exciting and interesting.

The story of color is a tale of humankind. Faber Birren's book, *Color, a Survey in Words and Pictures, From Ancient Mysticism to Modern Science*, offers an excellent account of early cultures' journey through color history. From the baffling cave drawings of Spain and France, dating back some twenty thousand years, where mineral pigments vividly expressed early hunts, to today's complicated science of laser paintings using light, color continues to fascinate us.

Besides natural phenomena, the earliest paints and dyes were made from nature's organic products. Records from Josephus, the first-century Jewish historian, described blue made from the gemstone lapis lazuli, red from the antlike cochineal insect, and yellow from sulphur soils and chrome minerals. Purple came from seashells, brown from iron clays, white from chalk and lime, while black was made from burnt bones and ivory. These colors were all used by early cultures for pottery, paintings, weaving, home arts, and even decorations for the flesh.

In the nineteenth century pigment dyes took a huge revolutionary step due to the invention of an eighteen-year-old. Henry Perkins discovered aniline dyes, derived from coal tar and carbon compounds, which led the science of chemistry to replace the old organic dye-maker. Modern chemistry now arranges thousands of complex carbon compounds, creating an almost infinite variety of pigment colors.

Varying in tint and shade according to the pigment dye, colors have different energy effects upon us. You may recognize the effect as warm, cool, weak, strong, high, or low. The bright primary colors give higher, warmer, and stronger energy than the soft, weaker, cooler pastels. Some colors are so bright that they create almost an unpleasant effect to our eyes, while others seem so pale that they melt into our skin tones. Some warm us when we're cool, while others bore us with their monotonous repetition. Over and over again, fashion designers advise the proper use of color to create the right effect.

Not surprisingly, color response influences many aspects of our lives other than just personal dress. Historical trends in color may give us a new insight into our culture's emotional state. Articles on the merchandizing use of color in the twentieth century have reported that in the United States since the thirties, there has been a noticeable surge toward reds during wartimes, and more favoring of light blues, grays, blacks, and browns during times of economic stress. Interestingly, art historians evaluating the mode of dress preceding the French Revolution have noted similarities in the colors and fashions used then to the outfits of the "flower children" generation of our late sixties.

Color choice may eventually become a futuristic indicator for people's sentiment during periods of change. Look at blue jeans. They became popular when the youth of America, concerned about the Vietnam conflict, expressed a need for security as well as a desire for more group representation. As our nation assumed more responsibility for its influence around the world, we saw dark blues become the national suit, representing the "executive." From the West Coast to the East, the "punk rock" colors may state a desire to be heard; the mauves declare a need for more sensitivity in the marketplace, and the new bright color designs of the eighties may express the public's need for more artistic creativity.

Myriad psychiatric studies have led to the development of art therapy, which uses color and form to help patients express their hidden emotions and also as a healing tool. As I mentioned in the introduction, one of the better-known tests developed to diagnose patients' emotional condition was created in the late sixties by Dr. Max Luscher, a Swiss psychologist. His book, *The Luscher Color Test*, once intended only for the professional audience, uses color cards psychometrically in sequential series of choice to reveal a person's psychological makeup.

The recent success of *Color Me Beautiful* attests to the fact that many people want to understand their personal relationship to color, as well as needing practical advice on how to use it. The focus of the book was external, offering the reader fashion and beauty advice based on the theory of "seasonal types" and their most natural flattering colors. I had the great pleasure of meeting the vivacious author of *Color Me Beautiful*, Carole Jackson, in 1981, when on a consulting trip to northern Virginia. I was honored, for I felt her book offered a superb color system for motivation of self-beautification—one that had helped millions of women and men to look and feel better by matching the correct shades of color to complexions, eyes, and hair. Her charm and colorful attire portrayed her mastery of her subject matter. Naturally, with our comradeship in the field of color, she was desirous of experiencing the SICA, which she did. And on my next trip east to teach a ten-week seminar in communicative and self-help qualities of color, she joined the class. Although extremely knowledgeable of color fashion, she had become more and more interested in the introspective and self-expressive fields of color, declaring that she would support my work whenever possible. A year later I was again to meet with this dynamic lady, for she invited me to be her guest speaker at a teaching seminar for her national Color Me Beautiful consultants. There she presented me with the opportunity of having many of the color counselors in attendance experience the SICA. We continue, years later, to travel our parallel courses to support the beautification of the inner and outer worlds of people through color, as color remains our medium of communication and exchange.

On the far opposite end of the color-conscious scale, New Age health practitioners prescribe colors as energy treatments for spiritual and physical alignment and balance. From America's west to east coasts, there's strong evidence of an increasing demand for the knowledge that these self-help teachers impart. Whatever the theory or practice, each marks a growing insatiable thirst for self-improvement using the common resource of color.

The Self-image Color Analysis, SICA, is designed to reveal your intuitive self-portrait. Whatever your favorite color is today, your personal discernment and color preference began when you were about two years old. Your likes and dislikes of certain colors have grown and changed with your experiences. As adults, preferences for particular colors are actual information coming from deep within our mental frameworks. Our color choices have established a personal language of our feelings—vitality, need, motivation, security, and fulfillment.

The SICA is fun—an inexpensive way of learning about yourself. There are no right or wrong answers. You cannot make a mistake. It will not decide your politics or religion, not even your race or income. The SICA system can only modify for you a nonverbal self-portrait. You can share it or not. But it can show you how you see yourself.

My book will explain exactly how to take the SICA. You'll

have fun selecting colors! You may even want to crayon or paint the answers. Imagine yourself an artist who's ready to paint yourself for you and others to see—a wonderfully encouraging self-portrait!

Before you begin your SICA portrait, find a working area where you have ample space and few distractions. Choose a color for each question asked, or buy a box of twenty-four crayons and lay them out so that all the colors are in full view. Most important, *do not intellectualize* or think too much about each color selection—spontaneous choice is the key to a more accurate interpretation. Let intuition be your guide! When choosing a color for each question, select only *one* for each circle. After you have selected all of your colors, you'll be ready to interpret your own image, and just maybe unlock some hidden doors for motivation and self-improvement.

The SICA will be divided into sections, your personal self-portrait and your personal environmental design. The personal portrait will be given first in the beginning of the book. After seeing yourself, you'll be able to select the right color to wear or design with for the right time or occasion.

You may want to select colors for both the personal and environmental SICA at the same time—do so! If not, do them separately. If for example you desire a quick insight into your image at a certain time, just do your personal portrait SICA. Remember, your color choices will change as you change, and as you focus on new horizons of yourself, you might even choose a new color, one you haven't used before. On the other hand, if you only want to change the image or color decor of your environment, just answer the SICA questions for colors and environment.

You'll find primary rainbow colors, achromatics such as white, black, and gray, as well as basic brown to choose from. Along with these there will even be a choice of gold or silver. Some of you may want more of a variety of colors, but don't worry about selecting the exact shade of the hue, for the more intuitive and spontaneous you are, the more accurate your results will be.

2

Your Self-portrait

Y ou are now ready to begin your SICA. The color analysis will be divided into *two* charts, Charts I and II, to help you visualize the image that you're communicating, and how you feel about it. You'll have a choice of *twenty* colors. If you prefer, you can color in your own circles with colored pencils, Magic Markers, or crayons. It really doesn't matter how you actually choose your colors—coloring them yourself or selecting them from the colors shown—as long as you choose only *one* color for each answer. You will receive no extra points for your coloring ability. But have fun and enjoy yourself in whatever way you desire to do the SICA. Of course, you may find the easiest way is simply to choose your colors from the ones displayed on the inside front cover.

Answer each numbered question with a color! Black, white, gray, brown, silver, and gold are not rainbow hues but are included because they do have color "meanings." I know those of you who are color sensitive will find it frustrating to be limited to twenty colors, but for the purposes of this book we could not contain *all* colors. The basic color meaning will *not* change greatly with varying shades or tints. So, if you would prefer a color not on the selection, try to choose a color closest to your preferred color. For example, if you want magenta, choose maroon; but for rust or brick, you will have to choose between orange and brown. And when you interpret your color choice, just look up both colors for a better understanding of you. For the more hard-to-pin-down colors such as plum, ask yourself, is it more pink or purple? For beige, read brown; for ivory, read white and then yellow for additional insight.

Keep in mind that your colors will change as you change. While your basic self-portrait (your *you* color) will probably not change a great deal, the other colors will. You might make a color change the next day. So you should do the test frequently, especially in times of stress.

Remember, try not to be *too analytical*; please be spontaneous! Let intuition and imagination be your guide. Use only one color for each answer. Read each question carefully; then let a color come quickly to mind and answer immediately. If you stop to think too much or mull too long over each question, your answers will not be as accurate as they should be. You're the artist, so be intuitive!

RED	LIGHT BLUE
PINK	DARK BLUE
MAROON	MAUVE
ORANGE	PURPLE
PEACH	BROWN
YELLOW	BLACK
MINT GREEN	WHITE
APPLE GREEN	GRAY
GREEN	SILVER
BLUE-GREEN (Teal)	GOLD

SICA QUESTIONS

Listed below are the questions for Chart I, and circles 1–7. Each question will have a number corresponding to a numbered circle. Pick your color for each question asked, and then match it to its corresponding circle. You may *repeat* a color as often as you like (especially if it's your favorite color).

Chart I is designed to portray through the language of color a portrait of your communicative image; how you see yourself and how others see you. It will provide insight into how you acknowledge yourself, your strengths and those characteristics you like to see in others. Along with people who complement your image, you'll recognize what part of you you prefer not to exhibit. And most important, Chart I will share with you by your color choices what expands and motivates your communications.

1. *If I were a color, what color would I be?*
   (Think of what color represents you. Don't be concerned about what color you might wear all the time, but choose a color that expresses you.)

2. *What color looks good with that color?*
   (See a color that inspires or picks up the color that represents you.)

3. *What color unifies those colors to work together?*
   (As a designer what color would you choose to help your first two color choices work together in a color chord?)

4. *What color harmonizes (has something in common) with your number 1 color choice?*
   (Think of a color that is complementary or blends well with the color that represents you.)

SICA SELF-PORTRAIT PART I

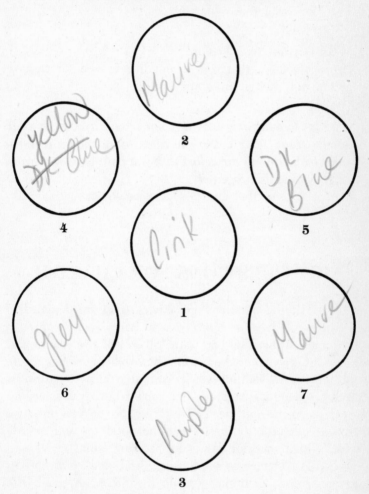

5. *What color contrasts (is different from) your number 1 color choice?*
(This color should be different from, but not in conflict with, the color that represents you.)

6. *What is your "yuk" color?*
(This is a color that you do not like to wear or to have around you in your environment.)

7. *Without looking at your yuk color (cover it up with your hand), study your color selections for a moment. What color motivates all the colors that you have chosen to work or go into action together?*
(This is a color that unifies your color choices.)

SICA QUESTIONS FOR CHART II

For Chart II, the questions and circles A–G are designed to help show you how in touch you are with yourself through feeling and sensing. This part of the SICA will give you insight, through intuitive color choice, into how well you communicate with yourself. In addition you'll learn your areas of stress, or your noncommunicative zones, and you'll see what you need for self-enhancement and greater happiness. So be very intuitive with these color selections! Read the questions and quickly respond with your color answer for accurate results.

Your colors change as you change, and your color choices may be different each time you do the SICA, especially the colors that reflect your moods and feelings. They can vary in a day, by a change of attitude, mood, because of a happening in your life, or they may remain the same if you're one of those very stable even-tempered individuals.

One of the surprises that you will receive from the results of

SICA SELF-PORTRAIT PART II

Chart II of the SICA is a new insight into the inner you, and into your immediate needs. By realizing what you're asking for in your life at the moment, you can become more objective with yourself. You will discover greater inner satisfaction. Most important, the results will help you in deciding what colors to wear and when, and will help teach you how to use the energy of the right color to enhance yourself.

Are you ready to begin? Don't forget, one color for each answer.

A. *How do you feel at this particular time?*
(Pretend that there is no language except the language of color, and select a color that identifies your feelings.)

B. *What color do you associate with thirst?*
(Feel being very thirsty and quickly choose a color that comes to mind.)

C. *When you think of something sweet, what color comes to mind immediately?*
(You can associate anything with this sensing, but name its color.)

D. *What color corresponds to roughness as related to the sense of touch?*
(Select a color that represents this tactile sensation to you.)

E. *What is your peaceful and calm color?*
(Close your eyes and feel a color that soothes and relaxes you.)

F. *What color relates to the most recent powerful emotional experience that you've had?*
(Remember for a moment how you felt and choose a color that identifies that feeling.)

G. *You have just heard some very exciting news! You feel great joy and happiness. What color would you choose to express that feeling?*

You have now finished both parts of the self-portrait SICA, Chart I, your *communicative image,* and Chart II, the *intuitive, sensitive* you. There are no right or wrong answers, and you did not make any mistakes. After all, you are the artist who painted your image in the language of color. It's now time to interpret how you see yourself. *Enjoy yourself!*

INTERPRETATION
FOR YOUR SELF-PORTRAIT

Your answer to question #1 will show you your color identity. The color that you have selected will give you insight into that part of you that you acknowledge and communicate to others. Read it, and then move to the Creative Profiles to gain more insight into the meaning of the color that you have chosen. This color selection will identify some of your communicative strengths.

COLOR 1   *The color that you have chosen to represent you acknowledges your image strengths.*

            You see yourself as:

RED   Ambitious, energetic, courageous, extroverted

PINK	Affectionate, loving, compassionate, sympathetic
MAROON	Sensuous, emotional, gregarious, overly sensitive
ORANGE	Competent, action-oriented, organized, impatient
PEACH	Gentle, charitable, dexterous, enthusiastic
YELLOW	Communicative, expressive, social, people-oriented
MINT GREEN	Modest, insightful, composed, kindhearted
APPLE GREEN	Innovative, adventurous, self-motivated, changeable
GREEN	Benevolent, humanistic, service-oriented, scientific
BLUE-GREEN (teal)	Idealistic, faithful, sentimental, inventive
LIGHT BLUE	Creative, perceptive, imaginative, analytical
DARK BLUE	Intelligent, executive, responsible, self-reliant
MAUVE	Delicate, reserved, sensitive, encouraging
PURPLE	Intuitive, feelingful, regal, spiritual
BROWN	Honest, down-to-earth, supportive, structured
BLACK	Disciplined, strong-willed, independent, opinionated
WHITE	Individualistic, egocentric, lonely, having low self-esteem
GRAY	Passive, noncommittal, stressed, overburdened
SILVER	Honorable, chivalrous, trustworthy, romantic
GOLD	Idealistic, noble, successful, having high values

CREATIVE PROFILES

Below are listed creative profiles for each color. Learning about your identity colors will help you become more aware of your self-image portrait. As with colors, there are many aspects to your pallette. Be open to yourself and the personal colors of your rainbow.

RED

For your identity color you have chosen the flashiest and most dramatic of all colors. Physical or emotional, "very human" is another name for you. You can be dynamic and direct but also generous. You, red, have a strong character and love to be active and competitive. You are solid in knowing what you want, and usually win.

If a female, you have a tendency to react quickly and emotionally, not always objectively. As a male who chooses red, you like to be out in front, often in politics, for you enjoy accolades from others. Some people call you a gladiator, some call you a leader. As a leader, you have the ability and energy to move forward positively.

You are red, you are first, the Adam and Eve of society, the sexiest of all. You have strength, courage, and conviction of your rights, as well as wanting equal justice for all.

PINK

You have chosen the most loving, yet feminine of all colors. Your heart and your emotions are your strength. As a light pastel, you are soft and gentle. Your weakness surfaces only when you know not how to close your heart. Yet when hot pink is your identity color, you become as strong as red. You may find your vulnerabilities in not recognizing your emotionally draining friends.

"Mama or Papa of society" are your claims to fame. Responsibility for others is your game. Because you are a combination of red and white, you energize others as the nurturer and rescuer. Lover, sweetheart, and rose, you assert love, the universal symbol for caring and sharing. Receive as you give to bring balance to your big heart.

MAROON

Like a ruby, your identity color is rich, rich red, the color of the sensualist and the color of the sensitive. Humor you have, for you enjoy fun and adventure, especially when the sun goes down. Your emotions are your strength. When positive, you always acquire positions of authority, but when emotionally upset, watch out, you can be volatile with anger or inflexibility.

You wear power naturally and easily. You have chosen the famed color of Rome. Love of life, and bounties of pleasurable things, are your banner. Your restless heart heals with play, laughter, and song, for your emotions require much expression to flow. Entertain and be entertained, for all the world loves you! Aren't you the color of burgundy?

ORANGE

Orange is a color of form and design. Your energy is high, and as a warm color, you are sometimes restless. Yet your competence and capabilities to organize are unmatched by any other color. An architect or engineer, a designer or marketer—you'll find your niche in these professions. You are the great self-starter and motivator. To get the job done is your goal, for your energy always requires a direction.

You like form and structure around you because you are very conscious of design. No messy homes or offices for you, for they make you feel "down." You flow straight as an arrow when focused. Like the sun at dawn, you give purpose to all who know you! After all, aren't you the resource fuel of life, the color of fire, the energy warmth for humankind?

PEACH

You have selected one of the most popular and social colors with which to identify. You're the color of a delicious fruit or the sky at sunrise. Gentle as pink, but action-oriented as orange you can be. Yet you have your own identity, that of a gentle doer or humanitarian.

You have the power to secure or stimulate the emotions of others, as you love to be emotionally independent yourself and have freedom to do as you please. You make the best color for classrooms and dining rooms, for children love you. Helping others to nourish and nurture themselves is your most attractive strength. Your only weakness is that you don't recognize your worth, as sometimes your pink or big heart gets in the way.

YELLOW

You have selected yellow, the color of the universal communicator. You love your mouth. Sometimes you talk too much, but all the world listens to your sharing. At times you're happy, at times you're funny, you're always good in sales. When you learn to listen, many see you as the great counselor, as you are sought for your talents to advise. The Egyptians and Mayans worshiped you, the color of the sun, for your power to sustain life.

You are bright and expressive and give warmth to many. You're the life of the party, the best friend of man and the voice of the country. Be the shining light for others. Hold on to your personal energy, though; it can be wasted, especially when your questions run away with you.

MINT GREEN

Cooling to the body and emotions, you are like ice cream on a hot summer's day. You have chosen the most insightful of all colors as your identity, for you prefer to use your mental capabilities along with your heart. You are green mixed with white, giving you the power of knowing what another is needy of, as well as aiding them to help themselves. "Modesty" is another one of your virtuous descriptors, since you prefer the dynamic reds to be out in front, not you! You don't deal well with strong emotional outbursts or loud "anythings," as you prefer to be left quietly alone to pursue your goals.

You'll be found in many alternative healing professions or just seeking knowledge to enhance your life. The asthetic harmonies of philosophy and natural arts appeal to you in a very special way. If one is to look, one will always discover you graciously serving without fanfare, hoping to make the world a little better.

APPLE GREEN

You have selected for your identity the color of spring grass, or a delicious green apple. A combination of pale yellow and green, you are extremely flexible and everyone's friend. People like you because of your open mind and adventurous spirit. You are usually found creating a new project or enterprise where you can quickly rise to the top. But there you won't stay, for you become too easily bored with anything routine.

Changeable, adventurous, and exciting you are, but not always sensitive to your own emotional needs. You like your mind to be stimulated rather than your heart, so you can go, go, go to the top. Your greatest asset is your outgoing interest in everything, from the stars to the rocks. Most of all, you like to enhance and expand yourself, to become everything you are.

GREEN

As a green identity, you have the strongest interest in the healing arts. You usually are found serving and aiding others in humanistic ways. Your compassion always surrounds the wanting, as well as those who are less fortunate than you. You have good perception and awareness about most things, but you don't appreciate sudden surprises. You're too stable to have your boat unexpectedly rocked.

When your shade is darker green, you love to be recognized for your superior mind, which enjoys details and balanced ledger sheets. Some call you a healer, yet some may call you a scientist. As a practitioner, your skills are unequaled, for you can usually see clearly into any situation. Health and balance are your goals, for you would like to discover life's hidden secrets, as well as return the earth and all its habitants to natural harmony.

BLUE-GREEN (teal)

The color of the ocean, of trees wet with rain, or the coolness of sparkling brooks—you flow with movement and self-contained energy. If you have chosen blue-green (teal) for identity, others find you hopeful, optimistic, believing, and trusting. You have more than enough of faith and hope, for you easily trust yourself and others. Professionally you'll be found in the helping arts of the mind or spirit, and often standing behind a podium.

Your contemporary acceptance in today's color world enables you as a royalty hue to give faith to others. Not green, the healer, not blue, the intellectual, but a combination of the qualities of both, you are! Some seek you for enlightenment, others for practical insight; for whoever seeks you, you offer inner calmness. Faith is your middle name.

LIGHT BLUE

You, the color of the sky at midday, are the most artistic and creative of all the colors. Imagination is your name. You love your mind and strive to express it freely. Sometimes it's hard to relax; you want to reach for the stars to bring them into form. Art, music, and literature stimulate you. When motivated to solve a problem, you have a strong creative sense of insight, as well as practicality. These traits permit you to enjoy a position among the great minds of society.

From the art world to the marketplace you'll be found, creating ideas, pictures, and form, always bringing in the new. You like to design businesses that serve the needs of the public, as well as creatively invest in new ventures. The universe has blessed you with its spark of imagination, so go for it, express it all the way!

DARK BLUE

You have chosen the color that identifies as the wisest of colors. Judge, executive, or business manager, you appear, for you enjoy decision making. Being very wise, you show good judgment of character. People respect you for your intellect. You are the favorite suit of lawmakers.

As a female, you have a tendency to be too independent and a little bossy. As a male, you see yourself so self-managed that sometimes it's difficult to accept advice from others. Yet you both are the universal teachers, for you love your knowledge and its authority.

Some people call you the boss, some call you the head. But as the head, you are not always aware of the needs of your body. You are the person who knows who you are and where you are going. Your balance is your heart, so stay in touch with your feelings. They will guide you to the needs of yourself, as well as to the sensitivity of others.

MAUVE

If you have chosen this calm, gentle color, mauve, for your identity, you are sensitive, delicate, reserved, yet nurturing to others. You have become the rage of the workplace; all women like what you represent—their supportive friend. Men are not quite used to you as yet, for you magnify their gentleness and intuitive nature.

As a male who identifies with the color mauve, you like to be known for your sensitivities. But you may need to seek a little more blue in your rainbow, for you are not always objective with your emotions and heart.

Some people call you the flower of the earth, or the violet rose of a sunset. As a color you have the ability to give peace to all. You are mauve, the new feelingful color of humanity, the most sensitive of all!

PURPLE

Purple or violet is the most intuitive of all colors. Like the amethyst, you are spiritual and thoughtful. Intuition is your name, for you are very gifted. Sometimes you're shy and hiding like the violet, other times noble and regal as the ruler. But always, you have high values for yourself and others. You prefer to look up rather than down. Because of your sensitivity, you have difficulty in trusting others completely.

Some call you spiritual, others call you religious. Whatever you are called, your faith will always see you through. You have the gift of feeling; not only for yourself, but you can help others to find their way. Always listen to yourself, for you are truly a gem of grace.

BROWN

You have identified as brown, the color of the earth. You are supportive and stable like a rock. Others see you as secure, some call you strength; you exhibit "lean upon me" properties. You always bring everything into order, for you have the gift of inner security. Honesty is your high virtue, as you have no time for exaggeration and frills. Your only vulnerability appears when you can't express yourself. You like to be heard.

Similar to the farmer and earth guardian, you find your professions close to nature. You like working with your hands. Secure, supportive, and dexterous, you belong to the country, for you are the machine that helps it grow—and the protector of the earth.

BLACK

If you have identified as the color black, you appear disciplined and protective of yourself. Black is powerful, black is mighty, but black can also be closed to light and openness. Sometimes black can be used for strength, sometimes for protection, but black can image a barrier between you and others. You may desire not to share but to stay locked alone in your world. Yet, you can be the favorite outfit to go anyplace or can mix and match with any color. You give a strong, authoritative image of yourself.

But if you've chosen black because of being despondent or down, open the door and let the sunshine in. Call a friend or call for help. You might just find a rainbow waiting with a pot of love and rewards.

WHITE

White is another achomatic that seeks to find other colors of the rainbow. When you choose it as your identity color, you probably are going through a transition. White is universal and abstract, a new idea without form. You are the ego, the individual, the wanderer, but forever alone. You have selected a simplistic and pure color, but one that reaches out for recognition.

Combined with the color red, mixed with blue, or as an additive to any color, you will change your hue. You search for your own truth; don't escape into your own abstraction. Come out to play. Join with others to make a colorful array. Some may call you a loner, but don't be alone, for you really desire a family and identity to belong to.

GRAY

You have chosen a neutral, named the famous monochromatic or achromatic. For superb contrast to any color, you are unequalled. Yet gray has little energy of its own because of its total passivity. You may feel tired, fatigued, or stressed today, for your energy is low. When you flow, all the rainbow colors belong to you as you set them to shine.

Play is your goal, and a vacation should be in the offing. With laughter you'll find more sensitivity to your needs, as you rest and revitalize. Some now find you low, some will see you tired, so pick up your color with the sun and sea. Don't be gray; be carefree!

SILVER

You have chosen a color of one of the precious metals, silver. Your sense of self-worth is high. Like the knights and ladies of old, you come to the rescue of others. You are romantic, for you always find the best in everyone, rich or poor alike. As a shield you like to protect others. But when you lose sight of your own worth, your shine loses its luster.

As a setting for most other colors, you make the best of friends. Your trustworthiness is unsurpassed. Others must earn your trust, though, for you have difficulty once it is broken. Rather than extending yourself out to the public, you prefer the limelight to come to you. Advocate and attorney fits your mold, for your "metal" can always be tested. You are the color of honor.

GOLD

Gold is the hue of wealth. You have a very rich nature, and in turn you make a strong securer for all people. In spirit, you as gold are the highest ideal and virtue. You enjoy shooting for the stars and settle for nothing less. You like grandeur, extravagance, and plenty. But your undoing can be your dreams, for when they are shattered or broken, you turn inward and attack yourself.

You are the best, you are the greatest, you're always worth your weight. Some may see you as fantastic, others see you as high-minded and proud. When melted, your strength extends to leadership or to support, for you are the awareness of the top and the dream for the future. You secure everyone.

INTERPRETATION FOR COLOR #2

Continue to interpret your answers for color #2, in order to learn more about your image. Your color choice here will show you where you find your source of inspiration. This color is your pick-me-up color! It always looks good with your identity color.

COLOR 2   *The color you have chosen for inspiration helps you get in touch with what you need to inspire yourself and to give a good image of yourself.*

You feel good when you:

RED   Get physical exercise, achieve or pursue ambitious goals, compete

PINK   Accept yourself, give and receive love, nurture others

MAROON   Have fun, and are adventurous and sensual

ORANGE   Organize goals, use energy constructively, are focused and productive

PEACH   Express and nurture yourself, demand equal opportunity

YELLOW   Socialize, communicate, and express yourself to others

MINT GREEN   Are objective, in control of your emotions, and see clearly

APPLE GREEN	Change, begin new projects, and are challenged
GREEN	Serve and help others, develop yourself, and see things clearly
BLUE-GREEN (teal)	Are truthful to yourself, follow your ideals, and be optimistic
LIGHT BLUE	Use your imagination, express yourself artistically, have creative outlets, and are practical
DARK BLUE	Manage yourself, are independent and self-reliant
MAUVE	Listen to your instincts, believe in yourself, and follow your inner guidance
PURPLE	Trust your feelings, use your intuition, are recognized as sensitive
BROWN	Are self-confident, secure, aware of your self-worth
BLACK	Are disciplined, independent, self-sufficient, meeting your own standards
WHITE	Have new ideas, creative insights, and an unregimented lifestyle
GRAY	Rest from stress, relax, remain uninvolved
SILVER	Seek truth, are honest, and recognize your own worth
GOLD	Pursue high ideals and goals, and reap and accept their rewards

INTERPRETATION FOR COLOR #3

Read and interpret your color responses for question #3. This color aids you in understanding how your best image is extended. It is a positive, securing color, for it will show what helps to balance you. Not only a key to better communication with your image, but one that continually helps you to stay in touch with yourself. This color should always be in your wardrobe, so you can use it as a color for balancing yourself.

COLOR 3   *The color you have chosen guides you to a better understanding of yourself.*

You bring yourself into balance with:

RED   Physical accomplishments, leadership roles, positive progress, success, and triumphs

PINK   Love, self-nurturing, emotional support from others, and being nice to self

MAROON   Sensual pleasures, emotional expression, music, dance, and dinner out once a week

ORANGE   Organization, productive use of time and energy, successful completion of goals

PEACH   Social activities, pursuit of community service, and active participation in charitable organizations

YELLOW   Self-expression, sharing yourself, and an optimistic attitude and smile

MINT GREEN   Continual self-development classes, involvements in New Age projects, and following beauty and health regimes

APPLE GREEN	New interests, challenges, self-regeneration, and playing of games of chance.
GREEN	Self-awareness development, self-improvement, and health and science pursuits
BLUE-GREEN (teal)	Artistic self-expression, involvement in church or spiritual groups, and quiet, creative play
LIGHT BLUE	Creativity, imagination, self-expression, use of knowledge for problem solving
DARK BLUE	Self-management, self-reliance, independence, and responsibility for others
MAUVE	Sensitive support from others, reliance on instinctive feeling, and time for meditation or relaxation.
PURPLE	Trust in, and honoring of, your intuitive inner feelings, and more time for listening
BROWN	Energy from the earth and natural elements, acquired personal security and self-worth
BLACK	Discipline, self-imposed guidelines, total self-reliance, and opportunities for independence
WHITE	New ideas, creative insights, a simplified lifestyle, and more time for self
GRAY	Rest, relaxation, lessening of involvements and stress, and a planned vacation
SILVER	A sense of self-worth, higher self-esteem, self-enhancement, and more trust of others
GOLD	Satisfaction from successful accomplishments and/or high attainments and goals

INTERPRETATION FOR COLOR #4

Your answers for this part of your self-portrait will show you how you recognize yourself in others. You can see how your friends and associates extend your talents and strengths. Like the old proverb "One is known by the company they keep," the color that you have chosen expresses another rainbow part of you!

COLOR 4 *The color that you have chosen for harmony helps you recognize more of your strengths, those attributes you like to see in others.*

Your best friends and associates can be:

RED Positive people, leaders, politicians, or industrialists

PINK Rescuers, nurturers, humanitarian benefactors, or childlike persons

MAROON Fun lovers, comedians, risk takers, or sensualists

ORANGE Architects, builders, market designers, or engineers

PEACH Humanitarians, club or organization elected officials, or community leaders

YELLOW Salespeople, consultants, counselors, or public arbitrators

MINT GREEN Natural healers, health food enthusiasts, poets, or beauty counselors

APPLE GREEN Innovators, freethinkers, initiators, or adventurers

GREEN Healers, therapists, humanists, or scientists

BLUE-GREEN (teal)	Futurists, missionaries, behavioral scientists, or spiritual mentors
LIGHT BLUE	Artists, designers, planners, or analysts
DARK BLUE	Executives, professionals, educators, or philosophers
MAUVE	Interior decorators, intuitive or sensitive artists, or spiritual counselors
PURPLE	Theologians, spiritual leaders, ministers, or philosophers
BROWN	Skilled workers, machine operators, farmers, or lovers of the earth
BLACK	Disciplinarians, authorities, dictators, or protectors
WHITE	Individualists, loners, or egocentric or lonely people
GRAY	Noncommittal associates, pacifists, uninvolved peers, or quiet people
SILVER	Crusaders, honorable friends, lawyers, or champions of justice
GOLD	High achievers or successful people, financiers, or futurists

INTERPRETATION FOR COLOR #5

This is a fun interpretation as your color answer for this question will identify who makes the best partner for you. Many relationships change as we evolve, and often we're not sure exactly what color (type of person) we partner with the best. The color that you have chosen identifies "Mr." or "Ms. Right" for the now! But remember, you're the artist, and as you change, your choice might change.

COLOR 5   *The color that you have chosen for contrast and support helps you recognize your most compatible partnership.*

If you are a woman, the man who makes the best partner for you is:

RED	A down-to-earth, sensuous lover
PINK	A father-type, or childlike sweetheart love
MAROON	A self-indulgent but fun-loving lover
ORANGE	An organizer and builder, motivator and work partner
PEACH	A kind and gentle man who cares
YELLOW	A buddy, friend, or mentor partner
MINT GREEN	A therapist, or practitioner in the health arts
APPLE GREEN	A new partner, or a change in partnership
GREEN	A medical or humanitarian partner
BLUE-GREEN (teal)	An independent but mentally stimulating partner
LIGHT BLUE	An artist or creative partner

DARK BLUE	A business or executive partner
MAUVE	A partner sensitive to your feelings
PURPLE	A minister or spiritual partner
BROWN	A steady, supportive, secured partner
BLACK	No partnership because of over self-reliance
WHITE	An individual who is a loner
GRAY	A submissive man who supports you
SILVER	A knight in shining armor
GOLD	A banker or wealthy man

If you are a man, the woman who makes the best partner for you is:

RED	A vivacious, sensuous woman
PINK	A mother- or daughter-type sweetheart
MAROON	A fun-loving, nonserious woman
ORANGE	A self-motivated, independent woman
PEACH	A compassionate, community-oriented woman
YELLOW	A social and communicative woman
MINT GREEN	An idealistic and comforting woman
APPLE GREEN	A challenge, or a new woman
GREEN	A health-conscious or healer partner
BLUE-GREEN (teal)	A mentally inspiring partner
LIGHT BLUE	An artist or creative partner
DARK BLUE	A businesswoman or equal partner

MAUVE	An intuitive spiritual partner
PURPLE	A sensitive and noble woman
BROWN	A steady, supportive, subservient partner
BLACK	No partnership because of overabundance of self-reliance
WHITE	An unattached, lonely woman
GRAY	A submissive or uncomplicated woman
SILVER	A romantic, trustworthy friend
GOLD	A self-accomplished, successful woman

INTERPRETATION FOR COLOR #6

Have you ever wondered why or for what reason you might not give a good first impression, or what your weak points are? Your dislike colors can aid you to find out. Your "yuk" color will reveal to you those hidden weaknesses or areas of your image that need more improvement. Your color choice for a dislike color will give clues in determining your vulnerabilities.

COLOR 6   *The color that you have chosen for your yuk color helps you recognize your major vulnerabilities.*

Your weakness shows up when you place yourself in situations where you:

RED
(such as: rose reds, fire-engine red, or magenta reds)   Can't control your temper or emotional outbursts and become angry with yourself

PINK (such as: rose pink carnation pink, or hot pink)	Feel dependent on others, or feel over-burdened by outside dependencies
MAROON (such as: deep reds, or brick reds)	Feel victimized or resentful because of the actions of others
ORANGE (such as: bright orange or burnt orange)	Feel confused, frustrated, or blocked
PEACH (such as: apricot and salmon)	Feel disorganized with your time and energy, or are embarrassed because of it
YELLOW (such as: banana, intense yellow, or mustard yellow)	Feel you are not living up to your own expectations, or are threatened by others' criticism
MINT GREEN (such as: pale green or aqua)	Feel unhappy with yourself because of lack of emotional stimulation or challenge
APPLE GREEN (yellow-greens, such as: chartreuse, avocado, or khaki green)	Feel that you can't express yourself or your opinions
GREEN (such as: grass, medium green, or pine green)	Feel bored or stymied because of lack of self-motivation or opportunity

BLUE-GREEN (teal) (such as: turquoise or peacock blue-green)	Feel emotional stress due to loss of faith or hope in yourself and others
BLUES (any blue: light, medium, or dark blue)	Feel mentally stressed due to lack of play and relaxation
MAUVE (such as: lavender or rose beige)	Feel that others restrict or are insensitive to your feelings
PURPLE (such as: orchid, violet, or grape)	Feel imposed upon by others' belief systems, religions, regulations, or rules
BROWN (such as: tan, beige, or dark browns)	Feel consumed by worry or permit fear or guilt to control you
BLACK	Feel despondent or depressed because of lack of self-recognition and insufficient love of self
WHITE	Feel lonely, unloved, separated emotionally, or detached
GRAY	Feel rejection, or fear or failure due to lack of self-acceptance or self-respect
SILVER	Feel dishonored by broken trusts
GOLD	Feel the loss of success or financial rewards

INTERPRETATION FOR COLOR #7

The color that you have chosen for #7 is a very important color, as it's the color that makes the best impression for a positive communicative image. In fact, it is your most personal communicative color! You might find that it can help you put your "best foot forward," expanding your image and working at the same time to motivate you. When translated from the color language to verbal language, you'll discover what your important motivation stimulants are.

COLOR 7   *The color that you have chosen for your motivation color helps you to expand your image and stimulate a positive impression of yourself!*

Your strongest motivating factors are:

RED   Personal recognition, power, positive attitude concerning your completion of goals

PINK   Loving relationships, responsibility for caring for others, and emotional fulfillments

MAROON   Emotional reinforcement, fun, adventure, emotional and physical play

ORANGE   Organization, goal planning, designing and building of projects, self-accomplishments

PEACH   Participation in humanitarian ventures and projects, being charitable, and acceptance of community-action roles

YELLOW   Socializing, expressing self, counseling, advising, and sharing in group activities

MINT GREEN   Self-awareness, self-health, and serving others in a humanistic manner

APPLE GREEN — New interests, change of old habits, new opportunites and challenges

GREEN — Clear insight, self-recognition, independence, and freedom of practice and action

BLUE-GREEN (teal) — Any enhancement practices for self-growth, freedom of choices, and better living opportunities

LIGHT BLUE — Creative or artistic projects or hobbies, problems to solve, mental games to play

DARK BLUE — Insights of wisdom, self-responsibility, knowledge, and management role-playing

MAUVE — Recognition of, sensitivity to, and trust of, personal intuitive and instinctual feelings

PURPLE — Teaching and preaching spiritual values, regal self-acceptance and assuredness

BROWN — Emotional and physical security, self-worth and self-trust, freedom from worry

BLACK — Total independence of action, self-sufficiency, authoritative positions

WHITE — New ideas to act upon, a more simplified lifestyle, freedom from outside pressures

GRAY — Relaxation, more free time, less involvements in daily stresses, and rest

SILVER — Practices of self-worth, honesty, trust of friends, and the value of truth

GOLD — High ideals, self-satisfaction in success, aspirations of high goals

Identity, inspiration, balance, vulnerability, motivation, or even partnership—all these parts of your image can be recognized by translating the language of color into words. Your self-portrait may differ from what you think you are, but take some time just visualizing it. You might see new talents, as you the artist have imaged it, so enjoy interpreting SICA, the game of the language of color. Your reward will be positive communicative strengths to work upon!

CHART II

You are now ready to interpret the second part of your SICA, Chart II. These interpretations will help show you how in touch you are with yourself through feeling and sensing. They will give you insight about the intuitive you. Your color choices will offer "color response meanings" for personal interpretations of your feelings and your sensing abilities. They'll show inner communication between you, the designer of your image, and you, the intuitive artist.

To begin, you'll want to know how you were feeling when you answered the SICA questions. So, we'll start with color A. Your color response will express similar to verbal language your mood or attitude at the time you were choosing or coloring your circles. Your color answer for A will not necessarily tell you how you were feeling yesterday or the day before, only *now*, when doing the SICA. Remember your colors change as you change, and your response may be different tomorrow, but it will help you see yourself today! Enjoy!

INTERPRETATIONS FOR COLOR A

How are you feeling at this particular time—an interesting question and answer for you. Your color choice will set the mood for your intuitive self-portrait of yourself. Like the artist, you've chosen the hue or tone for your painting! You'll recognize where you're coming from, or how you're responding to your own feelings. Read on to discover how you're intuitively feeling!

COLOR A   *The color that you have chosen for how you're feeling helps you to see the tone of your inner self-portrait.*

At the time you chose the color for how you were feeling, you were responding to yourself:

RED ....Emotionally

PINK ....Lovingly

MAROON ....Moodily

ORANGE ....With some confusion

PEACH ....Approvingly

YELLOW ....Openly

MINT GREEN ....Calmly

APPLE GREEN ....Adventurously

GREEN ....With some boredom

BLUE-GREEN (teal) ....Mechanically

LIGHT BLUE ....Analytically

DARK BLUE ....With some mental exhaustion

MAUVE ....Intuitively

PURPLE ....Oversensitively

BROWN ....With some uncertainty

BLACK ....With some despair

WHITE ....With some loneliness

GRAY ....With some emotional fatigue

SILVER ....With new self-respect

GOLD ....Materially

INTERPRETATION FOR COLOR B

Your answer for this part of your self-portrait will show you what you can use to expand your happiness and self-satisfaction. By associating a color with an unsatiated feeling or desire, you'll see how it offers you a happy solution.

COLOR B *The color that you have chosen for thirsty helps you recognize an inner desire, one that you would like to satisfy.*

My feelings tell me that I need more:

RED Physical exercise and emotional expression (Maybe a love affair or romantic interlude? If not, an exercise regime is a must!)

PINK Acceptance and love of myself (Maybe a special treat for me today, tomorrow, and every week from now on?)

MAROON	Emotional relaxation and recharging (Maybe a little play, song, and dance?)
ORANGE	Self-accomplishment and recognition of my goals (Maybe less frustration and more positive focusing on my career development?)
PEACH	Involvement in humanitarian projects or organizations (Maybe accept a leadership role in the school or community?)
YELLOW	Sharing of my personal thoughts and feelings to make room for laughter (Maybe a good friend or counselor to talk to?)
MINT GREEN	Awareness of my image, my body, and the power of my mind (Maybe a self-development or self-enhancement class?)
APPLE GREEN	Challenge in my work or play (Maybe a new job or new relationship?)
GREEN	Health consciousness and attention to my personal needs (Maybe a new plan for work, play, rest, and eating properly?)
BLUE-GREEN (teal)	Optimism and renewal of my faith and hope (Maybe an affirmation or prayer each day to recognize daily gifts?)
LIGHT BLUE	Artistic or creative hobbies for my self-expression (Maybe a little more insight into my creative powers through any art form?)
DARK BLUE	Self-responsibility and reliance upon my own judgment (Maybe *I* should become the decision maker?)

MAUVE   Recognition of my own intuitive powers and instinctual abilities
(Maybe I should pay more attention to my feelings?)

PURPLE   Sensitivity to my personal and spiritual needs
(Maybe I should try yoga or meditation to release my mind blocks?)

BROWN   Confidence and inner security, and less worry in my life
(Maybe I should work on trust and self-confidence in myself?)

BLACK   Self-imposed guidelines and disciplines
(Maybe a little more restriction on my wasting of time and energy?)

WHITE   Insight, perception, and greater awareness into myself and my life
(Maybe a little more openness to myself and to new ways of living?)

GRAY   Rest, relaxation, and freedom from daily stress
(Maybe I am due a vacation, sun and sea?)

SILVER   Self-worth, respect, and self-esteem
(Maybe I should accept myself more as I honor others?)

GOLD   Self-satisfaction from recognition of my dreams and high goals
(Maybe my goals are within reach?)

INTERPRETATION FOR COLOR C

Your answer for this part of your intuitive self-portrait will guide you to a better understanding of how accurate your sensual perception can be. Sweet sensations are pleasing to us; in fact, some of us tend to be "sweet freaks" as often we crave a sweet fix to satisfy any desire. Through the language of color you'll explore what "color meanings" are associated with sweet and pleasing to the senses at the same time. You'll have fun discovering how well your inner communication system works—a sense and a color working together. You may even discern that one of your important senses may tell it all!

COLOR C   *The color that you have chosen will help you to identify what you find very pleasing and satisfying through sensing.*

How sweet it is to:

RED — Be physically satisfied

PINK — Be lovingly satisfied

MAROON — Be emotionally satisfied

ORANGE — Have my appetites satisfied

PEACH — Be satisfied with myself

YELLOW — Be open to all my sensing

MINT GREEN — Be quiet and calm within

APPLE GREEN — Be able to self-express

GREEN — Have good balance and health

BLUE-GREEN (teal) — Be spiritually satisfied

LIGHT BLUE	Be creatively satisfied
DARK BLUE	Be intellectually satisfied
MAUVE	Accept my intuitive feelings
PURPLE	Be recognized for my sensitivity
BROWN	Be emotionally secure and accepted by others
BLACK	Be closed to my sensing
WHITE	Be separated from reality
GRAY	Be out of touch with my sensing
SILVER	Be out of touch with my sensing
GOLD	Be out of touch with my sensing

INTERPRETATION FOR COLOR D

Color D is your last color choice associating a color with sensing. The rest of the color interpretations will concern color for feeling and attitudes. But this color for roughness corresponds to your sense of touch and the tactile sensation that the color evokes. You'll once again recognize that you, color, and your sensing can communicate intuitively.

COLOR D

The color that you have chosen for roughness helps you to recognize what energy you do not find soothing to your senses. Your may consider it the color of an internal stress.

You respond uncomfortably to:

RED	..............................Uncontrolled anger
PINK	..............................Overemotional dependency
MAROON	..............................Emotional victimization
ORANGE	..............................Discord and confusion
PEACH	..............................Embarrassment or disgrace
YELLOW	..............................Unwarranted criticism
MINT GREEN	..............................Complacency or inactivity
APPLE GREEN	..............................Emotional repression
GREEN	..............................Loss of personal freedom
BLUE-GREEN (teal)	..............................Personal disillusionment
LIGHT BLUE	..............................Unsolved problems
DARK BLUE	..............................Mental exhaustion

MAUVE	..............................Insensitivity of others
PURPLE	..............................Restriction by authority
BROWN	..............................Excessive worry or guilt
BLACK	..............................Despair or depression
WHITE	..............................Loneliness or isolation
GRAY	..............................Rejection or failure
SILVER	..............................Dishonesty or deception
GOLD	..............................Loss of material welfare

INTERPRETATION FOR COLOR E

Continue interpreting your color answers for your self-portrait. Your color choice will show you how well you and your feelings communicate, and when you're most in touch with your inner strength and peace.

COLOR E *The color that you have chosen for calm helps you recognize inner strengths. These powers are an endless source of supply for you.*

You feel strong and emotionally secure when you are:

RED — Positive, energetic, and emotionally expressive

PINK — Loving, compassionate, and empathetic

MAROON — Kind, hospitable, and accepting your sensuality

ORANGE — Motivated, focused, and organized

PEACH — Charitable to yourself and others

YELLOW — Sharing, communicating, and expressing yourself

MINT GREEN — Composed, at peace with yourself and the world

APPLE GREEN — Innovative, challenged, happy, and healthy

GREEN — Serving and helping others with insight and understanding

BLUE-GREEN (teal) — Believing in yourself and faith in others

LIGHT BLUE — Creative, practical, and using your mind instead of your heart

DARK BLUE	In charge of and responsible for self and others
MAUVE	Listening to your intuitive and instinctual feelings
PURPLE	Aware of your sensitivities and believe in your own inner guidance
BROWN	Self-confident, self-secure, and understanding of your self-worth
BLACK	Self-disciplined and following your own directives and guidelines
WHITE	Open-minded, clear, and ready for new insights and new ideas
GRAY	Relaxed, rested, and emotionally uninvolved
SILVER	Trusting and accepting of others, and being truthful to yourself
GOLD	Satisfied, successful, and working toward your goals

INTERPRETATION FOR COLOR F

The color that you have chosen for F helps you to see, because of the language of color, your reaction to strong emotional stimuli. You permit this energy feeling to express a most intense part of you.

COLOR F

This color will indicate your positive or not-so-positive emotional response to a powerful experience. Look and see both meanings of this color. They might just share a little more light into "your feeling" and "sensing" energy makeup.

You react strongly to:

	Positive	*Not so positive*
RED	Physical/emotional love	Anger
PINK	Caring love	Overburdening
MAROON	Self-loving	Victimization
ORANGE	Satisfaction of my needs (such as food)	Frustration
PEACH	Championing for right	Embarrassment
YELLOW	Sharing	Criticism
MINT GREEN	Self-enhancing	Inactivity
APPLE GREEN	Innovating	Repression
GREEN	Physical health needs	Boredom

BLUE-GREEN (teal)	Higher faith	Patronizing
LIGHT BLUE	Mind expansion	Mental exhaustion
DARK BLUE	Decision making	Nervousness
MAUVE	Channeling	Lack of freedom
PURPLE	Social acceptance	Invasion of personal privacy
BROWN	Personal security	Guilt
BLACK	Self-power	Depression
WHITE	Little reaction	Separation
GRAY	No reaction	Fatigue
SILVER	Honor and ideals	Unworthiness
GOLD	Material possessions	Loss

INTERPRETATION FOR COLOR G

This is the happiest color choice of all! Why? Because it is the color that you have chosen for something wonderful. Your color expresses an inner joy that you feel. When you feel elevated and stimulated, you express this color and send clear signals from your feelings to your mind, expanding the image of yourself.

COLOR G   *The color that you have chosen for joy and happiness helps you recognize the happy, communicative you!*

You feel the happiest when you are:

RED   Positive in thought, in action, and in accomplishment

PINK   Loving yourself and accepting love as you love others

MAROON   Emotionally relaxed, secure, and having fun

ORANGE   Self-motivated, organized, and focused on your goals

PEACH   Sharing love and commitment in humanitarian programs

YELLOW   Expressing yourself, communicating, and sharing with others

MINT GREEN   Expanding and gaining insight into your own self-awareness

APPLE GREEN   Beginning new projects, adventures, and opportunities that challenge

GREEN	Helping and serving others to restore their balance
BLUE-GREEN (teal)	Following, acting on, and practicing your personal beliefs
LIGHT BLUE	Activating your creative mind as a designer or problem solver
DARK BLUE	Taking responsibility to manage and educate others
MAUVE	Using your intuitive insights as a resource for aiding others
PURPLE	Trusting and recognizing your sensitivities as gems of great value
BROWN	Secure within yourself concerning your inherent talents to provide self-survival
BLACK	Have control of yourself in order to communicate an authoritative image
WHITE	Open to new ideas and new perceptions concerning yourself and projects
GRAY	Relaxed, released from overinvolvements, and have freedom from stress
SILVER	Truthful to yourself, and believing in your self-worth and valor
GOLD	Stimulated by obtaining personal goals, success, and acquisitions of wealth

You have now finished both parts of the SICA, Chart I and Chart II—your self-portrait through the language of color. For Chart I, you have used your creative imaging to see yourself and to recognize your strong communicative strengths. In Chart II, you used your sensing and feeling about color to give you insight into the intuitive you. You might want to write down the verbal responses to your color selections in order to see your entire self-portrait—how you think you see yourself and how you feel about you.

In the next chapters you'll learn how to make your SICA portrait work for you, not just by analyzing your image, but by recognizing how you can put your SICA results to practical use. Try it in planning a communicative wardrobe, for a better image of yourself and for greater productivity.

3

How to Use the SICA to Improve Your Life

SICA portraits can only be inspirational if you choose to act upon your own unique qualities. The SICA discloses your talents, but you supply the action.

Your self-portrait can guide you artistically to a better understanding of yourself. It offers means for greater insight, inspiration, and motivation. Below are some guidelines to help you further interpret your SICA.

After you have matched the verbal responses to your selected colors from Charts I and II of your self-portrait, sit back and take a few minutes to get acquainted with the colors that you've chosen.

GUIDELINE #1 Look and see how many times you have repeated the same color in both charts— once, more than once, or many times.

Where, in what position, or with what number choice do you repeat the same color?

YOUR SELF-PORTRAIT

CHART I   CHART II

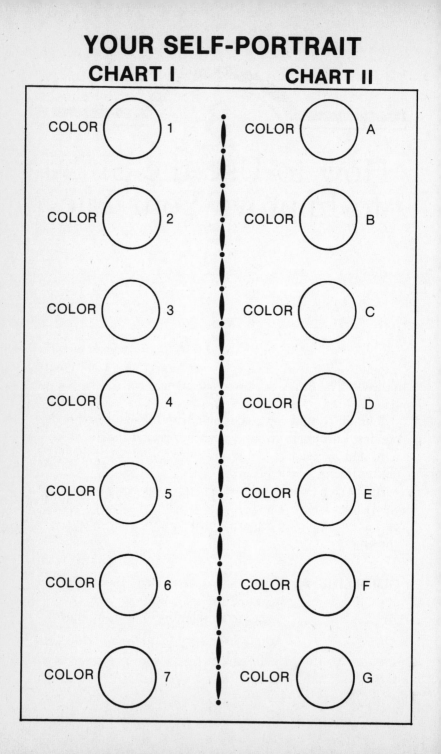

COLOR ( ) 1   COLOR ( ) A

COLOR ( ) 2   COLOR ( ) B

COLOR ( ) 3   COLOR ( ) C

COLOR ( ) 4   COLOR ( ) D

COLOR ( ) 5   COLOR ( ) E

COLOR ( ) 6   COLOR ( ) F

COLOR ( ) 7   COLOR ( ) G

Read again the "color response meanings" for the color that you've repeatedly used. This color should tell you something about yourself, a strong message from you to you!

Remember, you have intuitively chosen your colors, so your self-portrait is an individual grouping of your colors, not necessarily those of your friends, workmates, or members of your family. They belong personally to you!

GUIDELINE #2 Review Chart I, your creative image of yourself, and look at the colors that you have selected for inspiration (color #2), balance (color #3), and motivation (color #7). These are all positive extensions of your image, as they make you look and feel good. When you are experiencing any of these "color response meanings" you are communicating well and expanding your positivity.

The colors that you have chosen for inspiration, balance, and motivation will not tell you what job you should be in, but they will give you insight into what you like to do and feel good doing!

In the next chapter, Colors for You, we'll explore further how and when to wear these colors. But for now, familiarize yourself with your positive strength colors, those that you have chosen to extend your image.

GUIDELINE #3   Remembering the color that you've chosen for "yuk," and situations where you may need some improvement, permits you to take a look at one of your vulnerabilities. This personal color certainly doesn't make you feel good, and you should not wear it or have it in your environment. Since there are other in-depth interpretations for "yuk," do not focus a great deal on it. Rather, let the positive colors of your creative image be your game plan.

GUIDELINE #4   The color selections for Chart II help show you how in touch you are with yourself through feeling and sensing. They will give you insight about the "intuitive you." You will discover by your color choices what you might need to bring greater happiness into your life.

First, the color that you have selected for how you're feeling indicates your general mood or attitude. Look up again the color meaning for how you're responding to yourself (color A). The color should not need further interpretation, for all you have to do is to look to color B for your attitude color change. By sensing, you have intuitively informed yourself of what you need at this moment in time, your answer from color B. Your color response for color B offers you a happy solution for your current unmet need.

GUIDELINE #5   You might ask how do you determine what color indicates problems that you are having difficulty dealing with. Once again, by asking your sensing intuitive ability, you can discover what stress you find difficult to handle. Your color response for circle D can help your discovery. The color that you have selected aids you in recognizing your noncommunicative internal stresses.

In order to manage the stress, look quickly to color E for your answer. You are most in touch with your inner power with this color choice. Read the meaning again and again, or say a positive affirmation: "I feel strong and emotionally secure when I am _____."

GUIDELINE #6   The last color choice, color G, for your self-portrait is one of the most important of all. It helps you recognize the happy, communicative you, within yourself, between your feelings and your mind, and on the outside, between you and the world. This color can be used anywhere, anytime, or anyplace. Your "color meaning" expresses what makes you the all-together, happy you.

After analyzing your self-portrait, you might still want to see how others have used the SICA for their benefit. In the next few pages I have included a few stories on how the SICA has worked for others. You might compare their color choices, the color responses, and how they were aided by the SICA. All names have been changed, but the stories are true.

A HOUSEWIFE TURNED CREATIVELY PRODUCTIVE

I met Patricia, a homemaker, after a friend suggested that she have a SICA in an attempt to prevent further hospitalization. In fact, her friend paid for this first SICA and even delivered it to the hospital for her to complete.

Two weeks went by and a beautiful woman appeared in my office wanting to change herself, her attitudes, her image, and her general lifestyle. The report on the SICA had imaged her as "creative" (light blue) and her source of inspiration, color 2 (yellow), "communicative." Unfortunately, in her present home life these qualities were not being expressed. Her yuk color, circle 6, was yellow-green, which indicated she had no outlets for self-expression. She was having difficulty in finding a real purpose for living. She had lost sight of who she was. During the next year, after completing four SICAs and a month's guidance under a counselor, a new positive image of Patricia emerged.

Because of an early marriage and children, Patricia had never worked outside the home. With a new image of herself she was able to find a job as an office receptionist in a creative communications firm. She continued to visualize and focus upon her positive abilities. These brought her recognition by others and self-acceptance.

She is now an executive, independent and happy, with a career in which she contributes her skills of communications and creativity to a new self-awareness given to her by the SICA. This metamorphosis from an insecure, motherly, yet childlike, unhappy female, to a secure positive woman, occurred in a few short months. The SICA helped Patricia to find a purpose for living.

A BROKER TURNED MANAGER

At the time that John came to my office for an image consultation, he was a sales representative for a large financial brokerage house. The market was depressed and so was he. The SICA confirmed his feelings about himself. It also projected that his strengths to focus upon were his "executive" (dark blue), circle 2, abilities, and his circle 1, honesty and "lean upon me" qualities (brown). Others recognized his strengths, and he needed to image these daily to change his lackluster outlook on life. John enjoyed his SICA and felt motivated by it.

Being in a large boardroom of forty or more brokers, some with spirits down, had been a difficult environment for positive imaging. With renewed zeal he planned to move ahead. He imaged himself in new colors, wearing mainly dark blues and browns. He changed his environment to earth tones, even placing a large piece of petrified wood on his desk. He worked with his new insights concerning his strengths. Fame, recognition, and monetary stability were his results, circle B (orange), a satisfied desire.

Today he is the manager of the same brokerage house and a motivated executive to hundreds of salespersons. John is up, the market is stabilizing, and our manager includes gold in his rainbow spectrum.

AN UNDECIDED TURNED FOCUSED

A man named Richard was referred to me by a politician for whose campaign I had designed colors. He was seeking insight into himself simply because he did not know which direction to take. He was making various career choices in business and politics. His yuk color, circle 6, was black, yet he was wearing a favorite black suit to image himself. His SICA portrayed strong organizational qualities, circle 1 (orange), and balance with independent executive abilities, circle 3 (dark blue). He wanted a communicative challenge, circle 7 (yellow), and was desirous of change, circle B (apple green). His secret desire was to build and organize a new project, circle G (orange).

Richard found his new adventure, his new challenge, and a new freedom. He became leader, circle 1 (red), and communicator, circle 2 (yellow), of a political group where he could use his executive and organizational talents (dark blue and orange). This career change brought many rewards into his life, restoring his sense of purpose and self-satisfaction. SICA not only aided Richard with his own image (not wearing the black suit), circle 6 (black), but gave additional insight that helped him find a self-rewarding career.

A TEACHER TURNED BUSINESSWOMAN

Burnout—a result of giving too much time and energy without financial or emotional reward—is one of the main stresses of the educator. Jane had such a problem. She was ready to leave her teaching job. Her SICA showed too much giving, circle 6 (pink), and not enough recognition, circle B (orange), as well as strong aspects of creativity, circle 2 (light blue). What Jane needed was to wear less pink in her wardrobe, and to introduce more greens and peaches to balance her stress, circle 6 (pink). She was yearning for a creative hobby to stimulate herself.

After SICA, Jane signed up for an evening real estate course in the area. Although she could only sell part-time, she became so motivated with her new profession that she started her own real estate business.

Successful today, she not only instructs her clients on home and property buying, but she designs courses for inexperienced realtors on how to listen to the needs of their clients. Financially rewarded, her income matches that of highly paid executives. But her greatest reward is her knowledge that she is creative (light blue).

A SALESPERSON TURNED SUCCESSFUL

Carol had spent a great deal of time and money on books, courses, and tapes on positivity to enhance her sales career. After a job change from secretary to salesperson, she was seeking a new image. Other females in similar professions were wearing dark, somber outfits. Her SICA portrayed her in warm sunshine colors, circle 1 (yellow), circle 2 (orange), and circle 3 (gold). Unsure of how these new color selections would help create sales, she hesitantly purchased a new outfit in shades of gold. Her colors imaged communication (yellow), organization (orange), and successful accomplishments or high attainments (gold) for her balance. She liked her new image of herself.

In her first six months she doubled her production levels, and by the end of the same year she was chosen as the most productive sales executive for a large insurance company. Several articles have been written on her sales ability, her attitude, and her unique image. Carol credits the SICA with paving her road to success.

A STUDENT TURNED DIRECTED

SICA reinforces what we already know about ourselves. For a twenty-year-old college student, confused about his professional direction, SICA provided insight. Insecure, circle A (brown), and frustrated, circle F (orange), this student, Bill, came to my office for help. His profile showed positive strengths of creativity, circle 1 (light blue), and love of the earth and environment, circle 3 (brown). He was rebelling at the system, his yuk color, circle 6 (purple). He liked engineering, circle 4 (orange), but his major in college was English.

Recognizing himself through his color self-portrait, he decided to change his study curriculum. Now, with a degree in mining engineering and happily married, he has a career that he loves. His creativity (light blue) is expressed in development of practical uses for by-products of mines. His wife, a professional craftswoman in pottery, specializes in rainbow glazes.

From a confused, misdirected student to a satisfied mining engineer (orange and brown) who has found his inventiveness (light blue), this young man has followed his rainbow SICA.

A NURSE TURNED EXECUTIVE

Cindy, a nurse, completed her first SICA after an eight-hour shift on a hospital medical ward. Emotionally unrewarded, she was seeking change. In her frustration she thought that she was totally unskilled and unequipped to follow any other career except nursing. What to do was her question. SICA identified her as: a humanitarian, circle 1 (green), seeking change and challenge, circle B (apple green), and frustrated, her yuk color, circle 6 (orange). Her strengths showed the executive, circle 2 (dark blue), and the communicator, circle 3 (yellow).

She accepted her self-profile and changed her colors from whites, greens, and light blues to golds, yellows, dark blues, and peaches. Since her father had had a successful sales career, she began seeking a similar position.

A major corporation hired her as a counselor and a sales representative in their tax division. Her image changed from a "scrubbed too clean" female to a gracious, attractive person. Her executive peers were unconvinced that this beautiful woman was ever a plain Jane. Happy and successful, she found her humanitarian purpose and pursuit. Self-respect and a positive image were hers! She counsels others on how their image can aid them in solving their problems. Her SICA remains as the change agent that opened the door for a new beginning.

4

Colors for You

Now that you have interpreted your SICA, you can make use of your color selections for your wardrobe planning. Fashion designers and color consultants usually classify colors by warms and cools, by contrasts, by intensities, and by design and style. In this chapter your clothing colors will be given as "energy colors" to support you, who you are, and most important, to make you feel good.

Personal image counselors claim that a person's social/economic status can be determined by his or her clothing. So much emphasis has been placed on this initial impression created by one's appearance that a flood of information on how to "dress for success" is now available in books, magazines, and even videos. Empirical studies have documented that both attire and color make a personal statement, often adding to a credible professional image. Many researchers agree that a person's style of dress expresses the individual personality and gives clues to their probable social and behavioral interaction. Imagine how much more "successful" you can be if your wardrobe is expressing the real you, and not what someone *else* thinks you should be!

You have expressed yourself through the language of color,

YOUR SELF-PORTRAIT

CHART I   CHART II

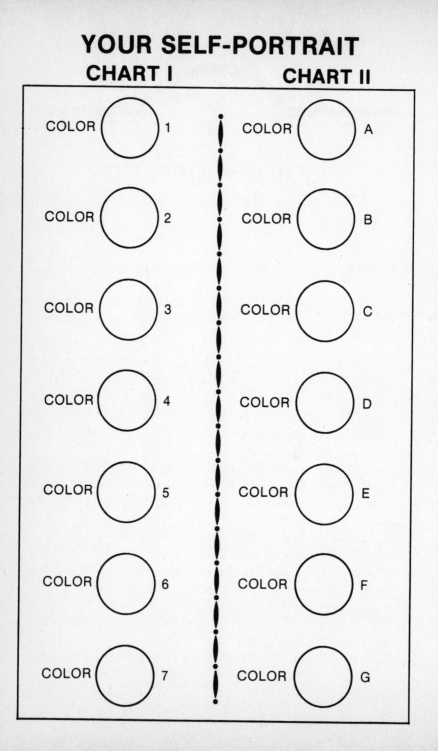

COLOR ( ) 1   COLOR ( ) A

COLOR ( ) 2   COLOR ( ) B

COLOR ( ) 3   COLOR ( ) C

COLOR ( ) 4   COLOR ( ) D

COLOR ( ) 5   COLOR ( ) E

COLOR ( ) 6   COLOR ( ) F

COLOR ( ) 7   COLOR ( ) G

SICA! Now, whatever you want to declare about yourself, your strengths, your feelings, or your creative talents, your chosen colors from your SICA can make that statement. They'll extend a positive image of yourself, give you additional vitality, and act as your personal resource. As an aid to work, they'll support your energy and stamina to get you happily through the day.

Always match your colors to your feelings. When you prepare to dress, touch the outfit that you plan to wear with your left hand. For a moment permit yourself to feel the energy sensation of the color. You can experiment each morning with this "energy feeling" and with practice become very sensitive to the different vibrations of color. If you have difficulty feeling the color sensation, try direct eye contact with each color outfit to receive the same sensation. By following these methods you will "dress for (your own) success." All colors that you wear will be positive energy, like sunshine to resource you.

Consider how colors react with you, day versus night. You feel different at your job than you do at home. Not only is it always smart to change your clothing and colors after a day at work, but it's also beneficial to your health and peace of mind. Color is like a stimulant, and you can overdose with it, similar to overeating. That's why it's unwise to dress anytime in just one solid color or to wear one color all day long. Better for you to coordinate your outfits mixing and matching two or three colors together, and if you do happen to wear one color all day, quickly get out of it as soon as you get home. Many people enjoy wearing solid black, yet without a helper color, their image is so strong and severe that there's little flow of energy and interaction with others. They can feel depressed or down by the end of the day. But wearing a little white, red, pink, or gray with their "basic black" will change their feelings surprisingly. Another common mistake is the wearing of total white, with loneliness as the by-product. A red belt, scarf, shoes, jewelry, or purse will solve the "alone" image problem, and the wearer will not only be individualistic but sexy too!

Learning to use SICA for wardrobe planning is very simple.

All you have to do is to select personal colors from your intuitive self-portrait and incorporate them into your outfits. To devise an easy plan for recognizing what your "energy communication" colors are, jot down a Color Clothing Plan according to your lifestyle requirements. This plan maps personal Colors for Work, Colors for Play, Colors to Present Oneself Positively, and Colors for greater Protection and Endurance against stresses.

COLOR CLOTHING PLAN

COLORS FOR WORK

According to your job, whatever it is—home, office, sales, or factory—you'll require colors that aid you to have a good day and be productive. You'll want to use your personal SICA colors to help you feel the best while extending the most positive image of yourself.

Start with Chart I of your SICA and select:

> Color #1 . . . (your identity-image color)
> Color #2 . . . (your inspiration color)
> Color #3 . . . (your balance color)
> Color #4 . . . (your extended-image color)
> Color #7 . . . (your motivation color)

In choosing colors for daily outfits, begin with your *inspiration* and *balance* colors. These two colors are vital in your wardrobe! There are many shades of these colors, whether muted or vivid, so choose from the varied tints out there the ones that are most pleasing to you.

Your *inspiration* choice, color #2, will give you a pick-me-up, aiding you to feel good during the day.

Your *balance* choice, color #3, is a support color, as it helps you feel secure and safe for the day.

Since you have imaged yourself as your *identity* color, color #1, there's no need to wear this color as your dominant outfit

COLORS FOR WORK
CHART I

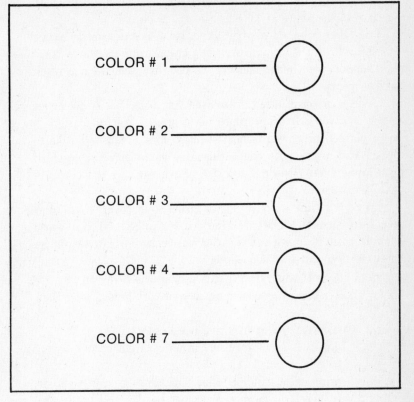

COLOR # 1 _____ ◯

COLOR # 2 _____ ◯

COLOR # 3 _____ ◯

COLOR # 4 _____ ◯

COLOR # 7 _____ ◯

CHART II

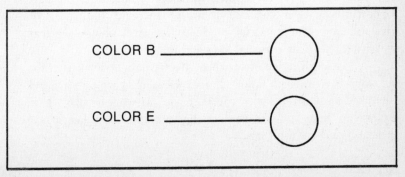

COLOR B _____ ◯

COLOR E _____ ◯

color, or to wear it all the time. You might use it more as an accent or secondary color to the major color of your outfit, such as in a blouse or tie.

The other colors of your SICA, color #4, your *extended-image* color, and color #7, your *motivation* color, can be worn to boost and support your image identity. So you may wear them as often as you please.

Once your have jotted down your five basic SICA colors for *work*, ask yourself a few more questions to help in designing your perfect-image wardrobe. "What colors do I usually like to wear? Are my favorite colors the same as my SICA colors?" If you know what "seasonal color" type you are, are the colors of SICA similar?

Take some time to look in your closet to discover what colors you have already. Or decide what colors can be used to mix and match with your *inspiration*, your *balance*, your *extended-image* and *identity*, and your *motivation* colors.

From Chart II you'll find that two of your sensing and feeling color choices can also contribute to your Colors for Work plan.

Color B... (your intuitive-need color)
Color E... (your intuitive inner-strength color)

Your sensing color, color B, may also act as a strong benefit, not only to give you more energy for the day and uplift your attitude, but also to help you to feel better about yourself. Color B, your *need* color is such a color. Need colors are lucky colors; sometimes lucky for love, lucky for success, and lucky for new opportunities. You can use them to increase your positive outlook and your personal productivity. And of course, this color adds to your personal satisfaction.

A good soothing color for those hectic days at work is color E, your *inner-strength* color choice. Wear it, keeping in mind that it communicates the "together you" at work or play. This color can help you use your energy properly as it keeps you peaceful and calm all day.

COLORS FOR PLAY

From Chart I Select:

Color #2 . . . (your inspiration color)
Color #3 . . . (your balance color)

From Chart II Select:

Color B . . . (your need color)
Color C . . . (your sweet color)
Color G . . . (your happy color)

The colors that you have chosen for #2, #3, B, C, and G are all wonderful colors to play in and have a good time. You might find that you have chosen the same color more than once, and if so, this color is "must" for your playful outfits.

COLORS TO PRESENT YOURSELF POSITIVELY

From Chart I select:

Color #2 . . . for outfit, or accent such as blouse or tie
or
Color #3 . . . for outfit, or accent such as blouse or tie
Color #7 . . . for accent
Color G . . . for accent

COLORS FOR PROTECTION AND ENDURANCE

From Chart I select:

Color #3 . . . any dark or bright shade of this color

As mentioned previously, your choice for color #3 helps you to feel strong, safe, and secure. If for any reason you tire of wearing this color a lot, you might want to choose another

COLORS FOR PLAY

CHART I

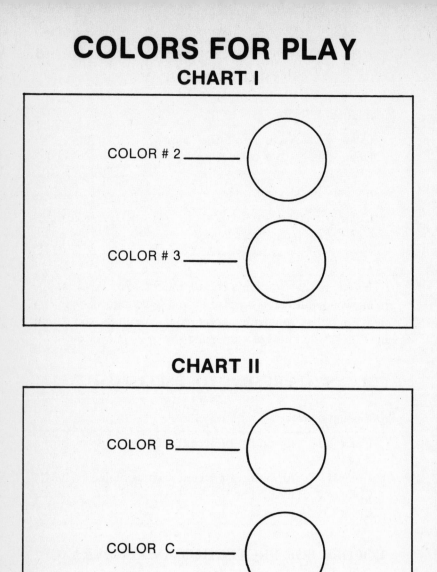

COLOR # 2 _____

COLOR # 3 _____

CHART II

COLOR B_____

COLOR C_____

COLOR G _____

COLORS TO PRESENT
YOURSELF POSITIVELY
CHART I

COLOR # 2 _____

COLOR # 3 _____

COLOR # 7 _____

CHART II

COLOR G _____

COLORS FOR PROTECTION
& ENDURANCE
CHART I

COLOR # 3 _____

securing color to add to your wardrobe. Following will be a chart of protection colors to help you make an alternative choice to your color #3. You might even want to select more than one. The choice is yours.

PROTECTION COLORS

Your protection colors may be used as your SICA color #3, your *balance* color, for they give added security when you place yourself in stressful situations, or ones that overtax your endurance levels. For example, when traveling short or long distances, your colors can aid as a source of protection from outside stresses and intrusion from large crowds. Many people become fatigued and stressed commuting on the freeways between home and office, when traveling by airplane, and on long vacation trips. Particularly for you salespersons who travel every week, your protection colors are the right ones to be used on these occasions. At other times you can use these colors for added support and reinforcement on the job. When wearing a dark or bright color, you will discover that you will feel stronger from the intensity of your clothing color. Instead of saying "I've had it," your protection color becomes your "I feel strong, safe, and secure" message.

RED
(Scarlet, cherry, or
Chinese red)

Counteracts physical fatigue

PINK
(Hot pinks,
magentas, or plums)

Relaxes mental tension

MAROON
(Wines, burgundies,
or cranberry reds)

Protects from outside intrusions

PROTECTION COLOR
I wear my navy blue suit to protect me against stress.

ORANGE
(Burnt orange, rust,
or gingers)

Balances confusion

PEACH
(Apricot, coral, or
salmons)

Protects from energy loss

YELLOW
(Honey yellows,
lemon, or sunshine
yellows)

Balances depression

MINT GREEN
(Aqua, light
turquoise, or sea
greens)

Calms down emotional stress

APPLE GREEN
(Celery, earth green,
or olive green)

Counteracts nervousness

GREEN
(Kelly, leaf, or
spring-grass greens)

Counteracts emotional stress

BLUE-GREEN
(Teal, emerald, or
evergreen)

Protects from outside interferences

LIGHT BLUE
(Bright blue,
turquoise, or peacock
blue)

Prevents emotional draining

DARK BLUE
(Royal blue, navy, or
midnight blue)

Protects against failures

MAUVE
(Orchid, rose plum,
or rose beige)

Reduces stressful worrying

PURPLE   Reduces outside pressures
(Grape, blue-violet,
or plum purples)

BROWN   Protects against insecurities
(Dark brown, sienna,
or earth browns)

BLACK   Protects against emotional oversensitivity
(Warm or cool blacks)

WHITE   Releases overburdening
(Antique or cream
whites)

GRAY   Counteracts overinvolvement
(Charcoal, stone, or
silver grays)

SILVER   Protects against loss of self-worth
(Metallic or pewter)

GOLD   Counteracts loss
(Metallic or gold
colors)

Whatever the shade of color, light or dark, the vibrations of color in your clothing help you. If you are concerned about how to wear certain colors because of how you look in them, don't be. For example, a pale yellow releases the same yellow sensation as a muted or golden yellow. If you're a person who has chosen yellow as one of your color choices in your SICA, and you feel you simply can't wear most shades of yellow for they don't go with your skin, you might try an ivory yellow. You'll find a yellow to choose from, so don't omit yellow from your wardrobe palette.

Don't forget that your *motivation* and *inspiration* colors can be worn anytime as accent colors. They may be worn on the top or on the bottom in external wearing apparel, or even as undergarments. There are so many colors in undergarments out there to select from, so you can even wear your inspiration or motivation colors without others viewing them, which can help particularly if you have to wear a uniform or have a dress code at work. You might enjoy adding other motivational or inspirational colors to your wardrobe to give you an added boost when needed. The following charts will give you more insights into their energy messages.

MOTIVATION COLORS

A motivation color inspires goals, enhances relationships, and stimulates greater productivity. This color may be worn as a gem or jewel, a scarf, a tie, or as an accent color to any outfit. Your motivation color will inspire you to direct a new flow of energy that expands both your image and personal goals. Motivating colors are ideal for pick-me-up days as they stimulate attitudes and feelings of self-worth. When you have those feelings of the "blahs," when nothing feels quite right, call upon a motivating color to change your mood.

COLOR	Motivates:
RED	A strong image
PINK	Responsibility
MAROON	Self-love
ORANGE	Action and results
PEACH	Charity to others
YELLOW	Better communication
MINT GREEN	Self-awareness
APPLE GREEN	Change
GREEN	Clearer insight

These colors may be worn as scarf or tie.

MOTIVATION COLOR
I wear my motivation color to get me going.

BLUE-GREEN (teal)	Independence
LIGHT BLUE	Creativity
DARK BLUE	Wisdom and discernment
MAUVE	Personal intuition
PURPLE	Regal assuredness
BROWN	Stability
BLACK	Strength of convictions
WHITE	An individualistic image
GRAY	A self-protective image
SILVER	Self-worth
GOLD	Material security

INSPIRATION COLORS

Your *inspiration* colors are those color choices from your SICA color #2 that make you feel "up." Creativity is the key for using these colors, as they are wonderful aids for fun, for romantic interactions, and for helping you enjoy yourself. Wear your inspiration color as a scarf, informal or play clothes, as an evening dressy blouse or shirt, or just anytime when you feel like letting your controls go. Enjoy and feel free, knowing that your "uplifting color" will do the rest.

COLOR	Wear it for:
RED	Physical restoration Emotional stimulation
PINK	Nurturing self Increasing friendships
MAROON	Rewarding self Being carefree
ORANGE	Self-organization Motivation
PEACH	Expressing yourself Feeling energetic
YELLOW	Better communication Halting depression
MINT GREEN	Feeling calm Feeling carefree
APPLE GREEN	Stimulating new opportunities Feeling challenged
GREEN	Stimulating practicality Maintaining balance

INSPIRATION COLOR
Wearing my pink sweater helps me nurture myself.

BLUE-GREEN (teal)   Promoting independence
Feeling optimistic

LIGHT BLUE   Stimulating creativity
Increasing perception

DARK BLUE   Protecting the emotions
Preventing fatigue

MAUVE   Stimulating intuitive awareness
Calming inner confusion

PURPLE   Feeling regal
Protecting from overindulgence

BROWN   Ensuring feelings of security
Stabilizing inconsistent actions

BLACK   Encouraging self-control
Promoting strength of convictions

WHITE   Relaxing tensions
Increasing individuality

GRAY   Alleviating stress
Relaxation and rest

SILVER   Stimulating self-respect
Alleviating self-pity

GOLD   Self-reward
Motivating high ideals

YOUR YUK COLOR

Your "yuk" color, color #6, is not a color to wear. You have rejected this color for it turns you off. Do you know that this color actually causes you to feel physically weaker and less productive? When you hold your yuk color in your hand, it might feel cold to your touch. This is because your energy is resisting the sensation from the color. Don't wear it, and don't use it in your environment. Even when you've found a good bargain on a magnificent outfit, don't buy it if the sale item is close to your yuk color. You'll never feel right in it!

During one of my workshops, an interested participant questioned how to handle a situation when one's yuk color is imposed by a dress code, or a rented apartment is furnished with their yuk color. You might be concerned about the same thing, now that you know that you reject the sensation from your yuk color. It is important to find a creative solution. In apparel, by wearing the opposite color of your yuk color, you can cancel any disturbing effect. A neutralizing effect occurs when two opposite colors are put together. For example, shades of yellow cancel purple, blues cancel shades of orange, and any white, including ivory and bone, will erase the sensation of overall black.

As for a rented apartment that contains your yuk color, try the same creative technique that you might use in your wardrobe. Opposite colors when placed together give a neutralizing or balancing effect. You can place a throw rug of maroon or burgundy on a yellow-green carpet, or you might use throw pillows of a blue-red color on your chartreuse lounge. Then add an accent of yellow to pull your whole color scheme together. Instead of "yuk," your friends will say, how lovely!

Below is a chart showing you the opposite colors of the twenty SICA colors. Look for your yuk color choice, color #6, then move across to find what opposite color balances or neutralizes it. Or you can look on the color wheel on the inside back cover.

COLOR WHEEL

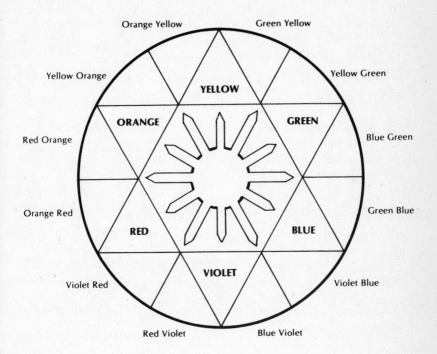

COLOR	OPPOSITE COLOR
RED	GREEN
PINK	DARK GREEN
MAROON	APPLE GREEN
ORANGE	BLUE
PEACH	DARK BLUE
YELLOW	PURPLE
MINT GREEN	CORAL
APPLE GREEN	MAROON
GREEN	RED
BLUE-GREEN (teal)	ROSE
LIGHT BLUE	RUST
DARK BLUE	PEACH
MAUVE	GOLD
PURPLE	YELLOW
BROWN	MINT GREEN
BLACK	WHITE
WHITE	BLACK
GRAY	NONE
SILVER	GOLD
GOLD	SILVER

Because many of you look so good in your "season hues" of colors, it's important to know how to blend your "skin tone" colors with your SICA colors. In Carole Jackson's book, *Color Me Beautiful*, she emphasizes learning how to select a personal wardrobe that contains shades of every color to enhance your own natural coloring—skin, hair, and eyes. Her concept of "seasonal color" offers an easy guideline for dress. A Spring shines with clear, bright, or delicate colors having yellow undertones; a Summer flows with soft blues and pinks; an Autumn looks best in stronger hues or oranges, browns, and golds; and a Winter sparkles in the bright, vivid, or icy colors with blue undertones.

If you know your season, take your color palette and compare your seasonal colors to your SICA colors. They should not be contradictory. The SICA is your "intuitive palette" and comes from within. Your SICA colors can easily be matched with personal shades of your "season palette." Your individuality and intuitive color preferences not only strengthen your energy levels, but they add to your fashion-palette colors as well. Be not only well-dressed, but learn to wear colors that make you feel strong, balanced, and secure.

Many of my clients have asked for color guidance on how to create a desired image. Fashion consultants, like most other professional authorities, often disagree on the exact methods of creating an image. Not disputing the theories of others, there is a simplistic method using only colors, not style or fashion of the day, as the principal designing rule. Below you will find these guidelines. You might even want to create some of your own, but remember, use only color as your tool.

COLORS FOR A DESIRED IMAGE

Here is the chart for coordinating two or more colors for contrast to project the image you want for the day, or for that special night.

DESIRED IMAGE	Colors:
DRAMATIC	Bold, vivid, primary colors, strong contrasts. (Combine bold and strong colors)

ROMANTIC

Pinks, rose reds, and pastels of all red and violet shades.
(Combine soft pastels, especially rose and pink colors. No sharp contrasts)

EXECUTIVE

Dark shades of blue, gray, brown, wine, and purple. All blacks with light pastel blouses or shirts. Bright color accents only with scarfs or ties.
(Mix and match dark outfits with the lightest of coordinates with just a dash of color)

SECURED

Earth tones and dark shades of all colors.
(Combine earth tones or deep shades of colors with bright accents of gold, ivory, or white)

INTELLECTUAL

Blues, blue-grays, and muted blues or blue-greens.
(Combine any shade of blue or blue-gray, with the basic neutrals, such as light gray, beige, or off-whites. Use stripes or linear designs in scarfs or ties)

SENSUAL

All warm colors (except yellow). Use light, bright, and dark shades, especially reds.
(Combine colors using a dominant red or rose red with flashy contrasting jewelry)

PASSIVE

Grays and neutral shades of gray-browns and blue-grays.
(Combine the basic neutrals, such as gray or beige, with other muted grayed colors. Avoid sharp contrasts)

PROTECTIVE

Navy blues, dark browns, and blacks only.
(Combine these colors with small amounts of primary colors for accents)

WHOLISTIC   Greens, violets, yellows, and earth tones with rainbow colors.
(Combine any greens with earth tones or any violets with golds or yellows or any basic colors with rainbow accents)

SUCCESS   All your SICA color choices.
(Combine your skin-tone hues with your SICA colors of *inspiration, balance, identity,* and *inner strength.* Even try your *need* color)
Be yourself!

Last, but not least, in addition to SICA's help for wardrobe planning, I would like to mention a color "support method" for stress management. The book, *Creative Wellness, a Holistic Guide to Total Health,* by Michelle Lusson, deals both with the physical and psychological levels of health. Color avoidance is one of the emphasized aids to this wellness support plan. The theory is that certain colors weaken one's resistance to stress according to individual glandular imbalances. If you're a person with physical problems such as a thyroid imbalance, allergies, or blood sugar irregularities, there are certain colors that should be avoided in your wardrobe. These colors further aggravate your glandular vulnerabilities, as they stimulate various personality traits, thereby overburdening your body's natural balance. For example, if you have problems with your thyroid, you might avoid red or blue-reds in outfit tops, as they stimulate a false sense of energy satisfaction, and less sensitivity to your own needs. I highly recommend this book for any of you who are experiencing a body weakness or physical irregularity. It should help you not only to know yourself better, but to stay healthy.

Experience now for yourself how your SICA colors and their energy qualities can be supportive to your wardrobe and you. If you've chosen a color that isn't present yet in your closet, give yourself a treat and see what your intuitive color can do for you.

5

Colors for Better Communication

Defining communication isn't easy; the scope is so great, the form and energy almost too irregular to lay down neat borders. My Merriam-Webster dictionary defines "communication" as "an act of transmitting; an exchange of information, a message." This meaning is true, yet there's no mention of the human-energy factor of exchange. The usual person-in-the-street defines "communication" as "Let's talk" or "Let me tell you what is happening with me" or "Tell me, what's going on with you!" This interaction is real, a true exchange of energy. Such is the interaction that takes place in color communication. You don't need perfect English, the proper words, or even the right thing to say, but you do require the best color for clear interaction. Colors communicate, they signal and send messages.

To accept the idea of color as a message transmitter, take a look at some of the more common, accepted knowns. Red says "Let's be physical," "I'm strong," or "Let's put our hearts together." Rarely do we receive a "mental" impression to red. Red often sends another signal: "compete to the end."

Imagine a boardroom meeting of executives where an important decision concerning company growth is about to take place. The attire emphasizes the individuals' unspoken attitudes. Around the conference table sit four men and two women. The scene opens. Two of the board members are dressed in navy blue, two in gray, one in earth tones, and the other in red. How would you write the outcome of the meeting? An objective decision must be agreed upon by all. Five of the colors communicate support, while red signals an emotional response. The wearing of this color may distract the other decision makers. In an important meeting, colors worn by attending members are of the utmost significance. They may determine the outcome, and in this case, the future of the company.

Yellow expands and when worn, opens better communications. Many of us empathize with the predicament of having children who resist attending new schools, beginning new projects, or participating in instructions for art, music, or sports activities. I often wish that when I had young children I had known about the power of color as a communicator. Yellow could have helped me, because I had a shy child who had difficulty returning to school after summer holidays. He just hated to make new friends. A yellow shirt might have reduced his feelings of shyness. Since he liked yellow and had some favorite tops in this color, wearing them might have helped him overcome his shyness.

For expanding your ability to communicate, try yellow; a yellow scarf, belt, blouse, or tie will do the trick. Yellow is the nonverbal mouth!

The favorite of all colors is the popular blue. In fact, in the history of color, the more technologically oriented a culture, the more people preferred blue. In these societies you'll see it as the number one car, the number one suit, and always, the color most preferred by men. Why? Blue, in all shades, communicates "I love my mind, and I like to be logical and practical." I theorize that blue is the color of the left brain, as it indicates intellect, not feeling. Messages signaled by the color blue always pertain to the mind, for it calms our emotions, which

COMMUNICATION
Let's communicate, in my yellow jacket I like to share.

then sets our minds free. The language of blue, then, echos the tone of modern society. In business situations, blue always gives strong support; however, too much blue on the body can have a negative side effect, as it reduces libido, our physical energy. Those of you who work in exacting professions, such as accounting, computers, or secretarial work require extra energy support for your bodies, not minds. Blue is not the best for you, except in shades of navy, as navy is a high-energy supportive color. Bright red won't help either, since it will focus all your energy on the needs of your body. You might settle for an in-between color to help you with better communications. Try a basic neutral with a bright primary color accent or one of your favorite earth tones with a blue accent. Remember, blue supports the mind for it images the intellect. But don't forget your body; you need it also.

On the following pages are two charts; the first will translate the *communicative message* of each color; the second will identify situations where colors present the clearest nonverbal signals. Look up your favorite colors and see which message they are sending. Learn how your wardrobe colors become better than a dictionary definition for "communication." And it's important; your colors are not separate from you; together you are one communicative message.

CHART I

Color Communicative Messages

COLOR	Message:
RED	"Look at me, I'm physical and emotional."
PINK	"I like to love, be loved, and care for others."
MAROON	"I want to play and have a little fun."
ORANGE	"I'm organized and like to accomplish my goals."
PEACH	"I'm charitable, kind, and like to be involved."
YELLOW	"Let's communicate, I like to share."
MINT GREEN	"I'm practical, calm, and like harmony in my life."
APPLE GREEN	"I like challenges and I want to be different."
GREEN	"Give me your sick and needy, for I like to help them."
BLUE-GREEN (teal)	"I'm always the optimist, and I have faith in others."
LIGHT BLUE	"Let me show you how creative yet analytical I am."
DARK BLUE	"I love to be the boss and the decision maker."
MAUVE	"I'm very intuitive, yet I need encouragement always."
PURPLE	"I like to express my feelings and have others recognize how great I am."
BROWN	"Let me show you with my hands, for I am industrious and love my work."

BLACK	"Don't tell me what to do, for I know best."
WHITE	"I like to be by myself, even in a crowd, for I need my own space."
GRAY	"I hear what you say, but I don't want to be involved."
SILVER	"I'm a romantic who likes to feel good about myself."
GOLD	"I want everything, money, power, and to sit on top of the world."

Color communication sends nonverbal signals. We exhibit our needs by the colors we wear. For example, one who wears red a lot might be looking for a new love relationship, or attempting to restore their physical endurance. You might ask if it's necessary to know what you want before you wear the color, as many of you have friends and associates who like to wear certain colors but have no idea of what they want or why they're wearing a particular hue a lot. To answer that question, you only have to compare nonverbal body language to the language of color. If a person crosses their arms while listening to a speaker, although they are unaware that their body is sending signals, a message is sent, one of probable rejection of the speaker's words.

A craving or desire for a color sends a clear nonverbal message too! It signals a want or need, one that wishes to be satisfied with the use of a certain color. As an example, when you find yourself overextended in time and energy, you might develop a craving for or find yourself wearing gray all the time. Or you may see your friend who wants to be more independent buying a new teal sweater. Both situations send color nonverbal messages. Color, come to my aid!

Below, you will find listed situations where color presents the clearest nonverbal messages. To use, look up the color that is being desired and read its communicative meaning.

CHART II

Communicate More Effectively

COLOR	Wear When You Want To:
RED	Bring in a romantic relationship Restore your physical endurance Express greater power Stand out in a crowd
PINK	Rescue yourself from stress Energize your femininity Stimulate responsibility for others Relax your mind and listen to your heart
MAROON	Reward yourself with some fun Stimulate a sensual relationship Ward off outside stresses Protect yourself from draining persons
ORANGE	Organize your time and energy Motivate yourself Bring in a desired result Protect your physical stamina
PEACH	Enhance your charitable action Support your energy levels Show love in action Stimulate the good opportunities
YELLOW	Enhance your communicative abilities Halt or prevent depression Stimulate your desires Sell yourself and your skills
MINT GREEN	Calm your emotions Heal your body Reduce outside drains Stimulate your romantic dreams

APPLE GREEN   Renew your desires
Motivate new interests
Stimulate a challenge
Bring a new opportunity

GREEN   Motivate your objectivity
Promote health consciousness
Stimulate an independent goal
Calm your emotional response to discord

BLUE-GREEN   Promote your independence
(teal)   Stimulate your practicality
Maintain spiritual practices
Reduce emotional stresses

LIGHT BLUE   Stimulate your creativity
Encourage your learning
Calm down overactivity
Increase your logic and analytical insight

DARK BLUE   Protect your emotions
Prevent fatigue on the job
Enhance your wisdom and discernment
Stimulate your self-awareness

MAUVE   Stimulate your intuitive insights
Trust your feelings
Calm your inner confusion
Reduce overactivity

PURPLE   Believe more in your faith
Protect from overinvolvements
Stimulate your intuitive abilities
Reduce outside pressures

BROWN   Ensure inner feelings of security
Prevent weight loss
Calm down excessive mental activity
Stabilize inconsistent actions

BLACK — Protect from outside influences
Release unknown fears
Encourage self-control
Promote your strength of convictions

WHITE — Counteract negative thinking
Communicate an individualistic image
Reduce your muscular tension
Be open to new ideas

GRAY — Alleviate outside stresses
Prevent unnecessary involvements
Encourage a self-protective image
Promote a calm, passive countenance

SILVER — Inspire faith and hope
Increase self-worth and self-esteem
Stimulate self-respect
Protect from inner fears

GOLD — Increase your material success
Motivate high ideals
Stimulate desire for self-reward
Enhance feelings of security

The subject of color communications offers one more very important transmitting and receiving avenue, one that gives us insight into our relationships with each other. But this method is the most difficult to grasp. You'll become your own analyst, so you are the one who sets the platform. Your *identity color* will be your player.

Draw a dircle in the middle of a clean white page. This becomes your sun, and the center of your universe. Place your identity color in your sun. Continue, with radiating lines to smaller circles surrounding your sun. Add the number of circles of persons in your family, or the number of circles representing peers and associates on the job. Now you have your personal or professional universe.

SUN UNIVERSE ANALYSIS

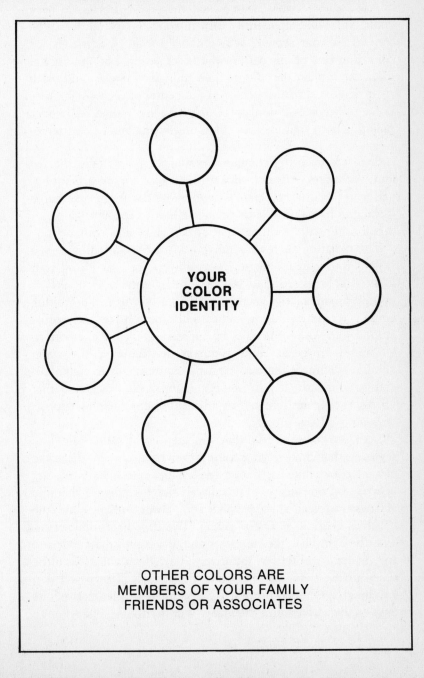

YOUR
COLOR
IDENTITY

OTHER COLORS ARE
MEMBERS OF YOUR FAMILY
FRIENDS OR ASSOCIATES

Ask someone what color would they be if they could be a color. This will help identify their relationship to you. It will be fun to ask your spouse, your children, your close friends, or even your boss or any person who has a personal or professional influence in your life. Target their individual circles, and place their name and identity color in the center of each circle. Your universe becomes a rainbow. Don't have more than ten circles radiating from your identity color, unless your family is extremely large.

Colors foster better communication among our family, friends, and workmates. Identity similarities, like colors in a painting, can work together to create a harmonious design, or one that is lacking in harmony. Colors can show how to encourage a better relationship with another, or they can show a discord.

The radiating circles around your identity color will give you insight into your interaction with others. For example, if your identity color is red, and you have other warm colors, such as pink, maroon, orange, peach, yellow, or brown in the orbiting circles, you enjoy like qualities and strengths in the people around you. All warm colors are expressive, energetic, emotional, and extroverted. Your common denominator, the warm color, represents a desire to express, and especially to communicate with mouth, hands, emotions, and body. You'll find that all colors that are similar to your identity color express aspects of you.

Let's say, for example, that you identify as yellow, and you discover that among your family two have chosen the same color, yellow, one has chosen dark blue, one light blue, one peach, and one mauve. Immediately you'll recognize that the yellows are communicative like you, always talking, and the peach is charitable, enjoys giving. The dark blue intellectualizes, the light blue likes to create and image with the mind, and the mauve is gentle but intuitive. The yellows will have to be quiet to listen to the blues and the mauve. The peach will readily give time to the yellows. The blues will let the yellows express themselves, and the mauve will need some quiet time to be intuitive and listen to their feelings. Then the yellows can interpret the mauve to the blues and so on. See how easy color identity for better communications can be, especially with a family.

Look up in the chart below the descriptor for the color identity of those you wish to better communicate with. If your identity color is one of the blues, you can understand other cool colors such as green and purple. You'll see like qualities in these color identities. Blues think and analyze with the mind, and they act out more subdued communications and interactions. Greens also like to use their minds before their emotions and mouths, while mauves and purples like to be quiet but use their minds too. What the cool colors have in common are like qualities of enjoying thinking faculties. But they usually need at least one red to keep the energy flowing.

If you discover that all of the surrounding circles are not akin to your identity color, you'll need to find alternative avenues to communicate clearly. Each color will provide a means for new insights into a better interaction. In color dynamics, a red always balances a green or blue-green, yellow helps purple to work more expressively, and blue governs or is supported by orange and brown. As identity colors of others interact with your identity color, they'll complement or stimulate you. If not, you'll just have to put greater effort into enhancing your relationships.

Below is the chart for you to analyze all of the identity colors in your "sun universe" drawing. Read the one word meaning for each color and you'll find a new insight into the relationship between you and she or he. Your "nonverbal color communications" diagram will give you greater understanding of how a part of you enjoys relating more positively with others.

RED ....Energetic

PINK ....Loving

MAROON..Emotional

ORANGE ....Conscientious

PEACH ....Charitable

YELLOW ....Communicative

MINT GREEN ....Idealistic

APPLE GREEN ....Innovative

GREEN ....Benevolent

BLUE-GREEN (teal) ....Optimistic

LIGHT BLUE..Creative

DARK BLUE...Intellectual

MAUVE ....Intuitive

PURPLE..Sensitive

BROWN ....Supportive

BLACK ....Protective

WHITE ....Individualistic

GRAY..Passive

SILVER ....Honorable

GOLD ....Materialistic

II
Color,
A Natural Support

6
Colors for Your Personal Environment

For those of you who feel hesitant about calling upon an interior decorator, or don't have the financial means to hire one, color-designing your own home or office can be a rewarding hobby. What makes a room really great is your personality and feelings of comfort. When it comes to style of furniture—antique, traditional, oriental, contemporary, or a harmonious blending of styles—all options are open. Your decorating will develop easily as you begin to feel secure with your color choices. In any bookstore you can find a variety of "how-to" books that describe principles for good design. But the most important rule for easy decorating is an understanding of how colors work to represent *you.*

Disregarding the "in thing" fashion color trends, you might intuitively select only those colors that are pleasing to your senses. As to the right use of color, *you* are the best decorator for your environment. And besides, the results of your creativity will be very satisfying.

Take a walk through your home, pretending you're a professional designer, and think about what style best describes the person who lives there. Bold, elegant, conservative, traditional, or warm—which expresses the mood and feeling you most enjoy? Does your home express that feeling? Look carefully at your favorite room. Perhaps you like spending time there because the colors make you feel so good? Have you ever wondered why your spouse loves his favorite easy chair, or why you sleep better on warm pastel sheets than on the cooler blues? Consider the answers to all of these questions—they will provide important guidance for your selection of colors. And remember, your feelings will be the most important factor in color choosing.

It is important therefore to use SICA, the language of color, to help you determine what your personal colors are for your decorating needs.

ENVIRONMENTAL SICA

There are only three questions to answer. As a guide to help you visualize the colors, return to the twenty-color selection display on the inside front cover. Also remember that you can choose any shade or tint of these colors, but select only one color for each answer. Again, be intuitive for the best results.

Color #1. *What color gives you the most pleasing feeling?*
(Close your eyes, feel wonderful, all your senses are satisfied. What color comes to mind?)

Color #2. *What color strengthens you?*
(Feel strong; everything around you is supporting you. What color gives you that feeling?)

Color #3. *What color makes you feel most secure?*
(See yourself as totally fulfilled; you want for nothing, you have it all. What color comes to mind?)

ENVIRONMENTAL SICA

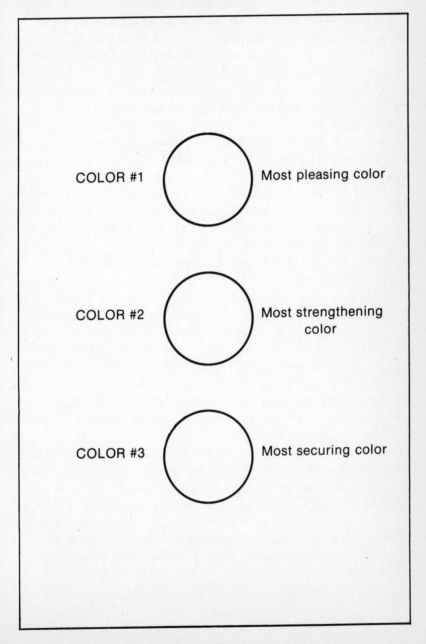

Once you have selected your color choices, write them down, for they are your most comfortable and satisfying colors. They will guide you in determining what colors to use for your home!

Other members of your family play a vital role in home decorating. Ask each one what their favorite color is, or give them the environmental SICA questionnaire. Surprisingly, you may find some members of your family enjoy the same colors that you feel good with. Be sure to include their color preferences in various accents, such as a couch pillow, a drapery color, or a creative ornament. Combine in your overall color scheme hues that represent comfortable feelings of all members of your family.

Read now how to use your environmental SICA colors, and those of your family. It's not important to translate them into words or communicative messages, for their "energy support" will be all that matters.

Color simplicity means decorating for comfort! Combine your three color choices into paint for your walls, any floor coverings or tiles, and colors of the patterns in your furnishings to set the stage for successful designing. For example, you might want to use a light shade of color #1 (your most pleasing color) on your walls; try in a sofa or chair to use your color #2 (your strengthening color); and for a carpet, choose your color #3 (your security color). Tie them all together with interesting accent colors that complement your entire SICA color scheme. You may even use for an accent color your SICA identity color #1 from your self-portrait.

Decide what you want your home to be—artistic, inviting, mellow, or dramatic. Then begin designing a room by using one color as the dominant tone. You can find it in almost every shade from light to dark. Use another in furnishings, or in an accent wall covering or in your carpet color tone. Your third color choice will tie the color design of color #1 with color #2 by adding additional harmony or contrast, or by simply introducing a secure feeling to the room.

If, for example, your environmental SICA colors are brown,

light blue, and yellow, you might choose any shade of brown or tan for walls or carpeting. Then add complementary blue chairs or ones having blue and golden yellow designs. Finally, complete the color design ingredients with yellow cushions or throw pillows. For added color complement, look to find a painting with sun, sky, and earth. Your room will be perfect, pleasing, strengthening, and securing. Or maybe you'd like to select pale-ivory or yellow walls with blue and earth-tone furnishings and tie them together with a luxurious blue carpet. Make sure that your colors enhance your feelings, or you won't be happy later on. Your favorite rooms need to be welcoming, but most important, very livable for you. After all, aren't your colors a representation of you?

Top designers emphasize, "Create your home as something very personal, the reflection of you." Your living room, dining area, and kitchen represent your image. Like the image of your car or your favorite outfit, the colors in your home speak.

Once you've reflected on your personal color choices, if you feel that there's still a color problem in designing your home environment, or you're not quite satisfied with your "feeling" colors, there are alternative ways to solve the problem using your personal self-portrait, SICA.

Return to your self-portrait and study the colors that you have chosen for Chart I. Ask yourself, "Do I like the colors that I have chosen for Chart I?" Could you pick just three of them for decorating your home? After all, they are colors that extend your image. You may prefer them in your home as well. If you don't favor your "feeling" colors, try your image colors, they'll work too. But don't use your yuk color in your home!

Another easy method for choosing colors for your home is to join with your spouse or friend, or whoever is your homemate, in selecting a painting or art design that has in its composition or subject matter colors that you both like and can live happily with. Ask yourselves if these colors please you and make you feel secure. Then choose three of the colors from the art piece for your personal color scheme in designing your home. Build those "pleasing feelings" around the color of the art that you enjoy!

I have an interesting story to relate about a color design problem involving a married couple, and how it was solved.

A few years ago a young lady telephoned the office, wanting to know if I could aid her in resolving a stressful situation. Apparently she and her husband had recently purchased a home, but they were unable to arrive at a mutual agreement concerning a basic color scheme for decorating. The husband's favorite color was blue, and he expressed a strong dislike for anything green. Her problem was that she loved greens and disliked blues. This problem typically occurs when people enter a new cycle of their lives, such as buying a new home. A seemingly small choice becomes a monumental obstacle.

The results of their joint participation in the SICA were revealing. The husband did indeed identify with shades of blue; his yuk color was green; while his wife, including her professional image, identified as green and suffered discomfort with too much blue. The key that opened the door for a happy decision was the color gold. Both parties chose gold for security and feelings of comfort. The interior design color scheme was then decided quite simply. A gold carpet throughout the home, antique off-white walls with golden highlights, furnishings coordinating golden yellows, muted green-blues, woods, straws, and green plants brought about the settlement of their differences. Indeed, their gratitude and pleasure remained in the aura of my office for many days.

Now you're ready to work with your colors to decorate. Read some of the helpful hints for color decorating in the chart below, and become your own master designer. If you still feel unsure of yourself, ask for guidance from a professional, but don't forget your personal colors—they represent you!

SIMPLE WAYS TO COLOR DECORATE

Here are a few ways to enjoy your favorite colors in individual rooms without struggling over design decisions. Start by creating a small room that you enjoy. Have your SICA colors offer their "energy," while delighting your eyes at the same time.

1. Design 60 percent of the room—walls and floor, whether it be carpet, tile, or wood—in various tints and shades of *one* favorite color.

2. Make 30 percent of the room—draperies and upholstered furniture—tints and shades of your *second* favorite color.

3. Accent the final 10 percent of the room—with pictures, vases, pillows—in colors to please and support all members of your household.

4. Repeat colors to unify a room or tie one room to another, for these colors if carried throughout the entire home later will build a coordinated image.

5. Remember, woods and other natural products are colors. Wood-tones, fibers, bricks, or stones are all part of your color scheme, as they are part of the total picture of any room.

6. The lighting, both natural and artificial, in the room that you are designing affects your colors. Colors look different under daylight than they do under various kinds of artificial light or night lighting. Warm lights cause your warm colors to appear warmer, while cool lights will make your colors seem grayer; and the opposite will happen with your cool colors. If the rooms that you are decorating are very dark, do not choose your colors outside or in better-lit rooms. Rather, select the colors in the exact room to be designed.

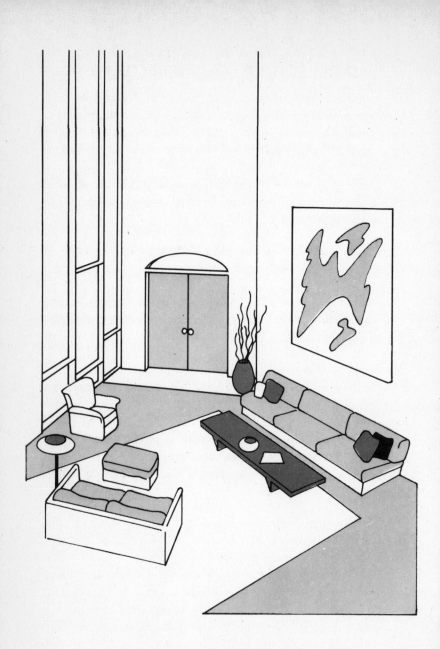

A well-designed room using three colors for
pleasure, support and security.

7. Bright, bold primary colors, such as red, yellow, and bright blues, decrease the size of rooms. You might use these colors more for accents or in smaller pieces of furniture.

8. Light and pastel colors make a room look larger and lighter. You may want to use these colors for smaller rooms and areas. Pastel colors also help you relax.

9. White is a color and should be considered as one of your three design colors. Remember, if you design with all white, your room can be lonely, so add two more colors to make it sparkle.

10. Use at least two different colors together in any room to create contrast. When you use a small amount of contrast with shades of the same hue or color, your room will be more restful and calm, as well as airy.

11. Warm colors such as reds, yellows, oranges, and browns create warmer atmospheres in a room, conserving heat and electricity. Cool colors, such as blues, purples, and grays, chill down the temperature of the room and can be used as natural air conditioners. Warning: too much blue in any room might cause you to want to wear a sweater!

Be creative and enjoy a well-designed home.

COLORS FOR SPECIAL ENVIRONMENTS

You may want added knowledge on how to design nurseries, children's rooms, or rooms for the elderly. If you feel that a room requires particular attention in decorating, it is a special environment!

Let's address special environments one at a time, and if you find the information helpful to your personal requirements, try experimenting with it.

1) *From your child's birth until it is about age seven*, you, Mom, or you, Dad, are the designer. Your responsibility is not to overactivate your child's nursery or room with color choice and bold contrasts. Bright, intense colors, such as bright reds, oranges, and strong yellows, can be overstimulating, while light yellow, peach, or pink are more suitable, for they are soothing and comfortable. Greens are calming and cooling, yet are not always advisable for chilly rooms or for nurseries where baby is susceptible to colic or colds. It's true, blue has been identified as the color for little boys, yet some blues are so cool that they can make a newborn feel the cold more. You can use blues positively to aid an overactive child, but don't count on it to offer much physical or emotional support. Try one of the other colors on the walls of your son's room with blue accents of furnishings and trims. In this way the room says "boy child" but doesn't overdose with the cooling blues.

When you don't know your child's gender before birth, select a light yellow and after the child is born, add a few bright accents for his/her identity. Your baby reacts favorably to soft light when born and grows in sensitivity to surrounding colors as he/she develops. Be communicative and warm with your young child, and later on in life, they will let you know how much they care.

2) *From age seven to age fourteen*, you, Mom and Dad, are the designers, with your child as your major consultant. Ask your child what his favorite color is, and what color makes him feel the best. Share his color wants and encourage him to enjoy designing his room. If your son enjoys pink or purple, and your reaction is that it's not okay, don't feel that way, for your child is requesting a color for a reason. Agree and acknowledge him. Shy, sensitive children of either sex love the gentle, intuitive colors. On the other hand, if your "tomboy girl" is into bright reds and blues, recognize that she too wants her personal colors, and they're right for her. She may be asking for more color support to help her grow bright and strong.

3) *From age seventy to whatever*, you, as a respected senior, always require extra color balancing and support. Especially when your feet are cold or you're having a down day, you can call upon color to aid. Warm colors control cool environments, while the soft yellows and salmons also prevent loneliness or depression. The myth that the elderly prefer violet is just that, a misbelief. In fact, violet or mauve is not the best choice for a senior citizen as it can cause an elderly person to become overly introspective and moody. For walls and accents in furnishings, the best colors are light pinks, salmons, yellows, blue-greens, and beiges. They can all work as helpers to promote comfort and security. So when one's hair turns to white, it's time to use more color in the environment.

4) *The most influential room* to give special attention to is the bathroom. Romans and Greeks understood the attributes of the bath, that of rejuvenation and restoration. Think about it. Don't you enjoy spending time there, maybe even hours soaking and pampering? Your day begins in the bathroom. In order to get a good start there, make sure the colors are uplifting. Turn your bathroom into a magic spa for repairing that body of yours, and rejuvenating and putting on your face for the day. Your colors should inspire you as you get your first look at yourself. Instead

of peering into your mirror with a long face, let your bathroom colors serve as your first "pick-me-up."

Naturally, when choosing the principal color for your bathroom, start with an inspiring color. Use any tint or shade of this color. Design the accents of your bathroom with colors that represent other family members or associates, so that they will feel good as you do. Listed below is a simple chart for inspiring colors.

COLOR FOR BATHROOM DESIGNING

RED — Cherry, scarlet, or Chinese red - (PHYSICAL)

PINK — All pinks, hot pinks, and plums - (ROMANTIC)

MAROON — Wines, burgundies, or cranberry reds - (SENSUAL)

ORANGE — Tangerines, orange, or burnt orange - (STRUCTURED)

PEACH — Apricot, peach, or salmon - (EMOTIONALLY SUPPORTIVE)

YELLOW — Lemon or sunshine, and honey yellows - (CHEERY)

MINT GREEN — Sea green, mint, or aquas - (SOOTHING)

APPLE GREEN — Celery, grass, apple or nile greens - (EXCITING)

GREEN — Emerald, kelly or leaf greens - (HEALING)

BLUE-GREEN — Teal, ocean, or evergreens - (PEACEFUL)

LIGHT BLUE — Turquoise, baby or peacock blues - (SERENE)

DARK BLUE | Royal blue, navy or midnight blues - (EXECUTIVE)

MAUVE | Orchid, rose plum, or rose beiges - (FEELINGFUL)

PURPLE | Grape, blue-violet, or plum purples - (DIGNIFIED)

BROWN | Beige, tan, sienna, or earth browns - (SECURING)

BLACK | All shades of black - (MODERN, but SEVERE)

WHITE | All shades of white - (UNCLUTTERED, but STERILE)

GRAY | Stone or silver and charcoal grays - (RESTFUL)

SILVER | Metallic or pewter silvers - (LUXURIOUS)

GOLD | Metallic or gold colors - (ELEGANT)

CHROMATIC PLANNING FOR
JOB SUPPORT

Have you ever gone to work and wondered what you could do to have your job environment be more congenial and satisfying? Perhaps you've bought something new for your desk to liven it up a bit. Most of you who work for government or big business, or even services and sales organizations, have had little or no voice in designing your job environments. Fortunately there's growing interest among businesses to change the work environment, to include the needs of the employees and to make the surroundings more pleasing and efficient.

Home and office, like shelter and open space, often don't have the same focus of performance or purpose. When at home, we rest, relax, rejuvenate, and create, while on the job we work, produce, serve, and solve job-related problems, resting little if at all. Our "energy" is consumed more at work than at home. This is not quite so true with many homemakers, since their role as mother or father requires the same endurance level as a full-time job. Wherever your energy is mostly spent, you could use a little extra help from the colors in your environment.

It's essential in order to receive the most benefit from your personal colors to place them somewhere within three feet of your working space. On a table, a desk, a chair, in a piece of art, or as an accent color, anywhere in view—for your colors can act as strong energy to help you feel good and produce your best at work.

You might select your personal colors from your SICA self-portrait, color #2, your inspiration color, and color #3, your balance or security color. For example, if your balance color is maroon, you can use it in your office as your desk chair, a wallpaper design, a small area rug, or even as a figurine on your desk. If it's not possible to have a say in the colors of your work environment, carry an object of maroon with you, like a pen that you can place on your desk while at work. Any object at all in a maroon color can serve as your balance color to help you feel better on the job. Try even a maroon scratch-pad holder, an ink blotter, or maroon vase. To gain the "energy effect" from your personal color, you don't have to have a lot of it, just a small amount to energize you through the day.

Your inspiration color, #2 from your SICA, may be another color you wish to include in your work environment. Let's suppose that you've chosen yellow. You can have it as a tablet, a book, a planter, a name tag, a favorite coffee mug, or any piece of office equipment around you. Like a friend, the color yellow will support you to be more communicative and inspired while at work.

Some of my clients have asked what to do when their work environment is color-designed in their yuk color. Unfortunately this often happens and makes for a critical and immediate need for the resolution to the problem. The best way to handle your yuk color is to hastily add in your work space personal colors for additional support, and you should wear colors that neutralize the energy effect of your dislike color. Refer back to the chapter Colors for You, to the section Your Yuk Color (page 94), and read how to cancel the effect of the color with its opposite. Sadly, you may have to wear a lot of the same color outfits, but at least you'll be feeling fine and producing at work.

Last but not least in this chapter, for all you business owners or entrepreneurs who might want to image your service or your products with communicative impressions from the meanings of colors, below is a list of colors for services and marketing. These, along with your personal SICA colors, may be used as accents, business cards, logos, signs, or creative designs for your company. Here are some definitions and examples of color-imaging.

YOUR SELF-PORTRAIT

CHART I   CHART II

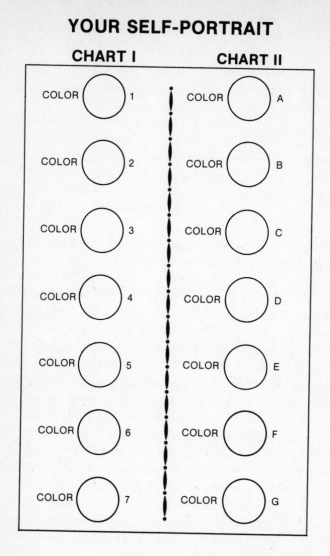

COLOR	1	COLOR	A
COLOR	2	COLOR	B
COLOR	3	COLOR	C
COLOR	4	COLOR	D
COLOR	5	COLOR	E
COLOR	6	COLOR	F
COLOR	7	COLOR	G

COLOR

RED

Service or Product Pertaining to:

PHYSICAL IMAGING
(Sports, exercise clubs, dining or
dancing services, political clubs and
organizations)

PINK	A FEMININE OR LOVING IMAGE (Fashions, cosmetics, rescuing services, church clubs, and infant services and products)
MAROON	GRATIFICATION OF THE SENSES (Entertainment, videos, cars, furnishings, art services, gambling, and beverages)
ORANGE	HIGH-ENERGY IMAGES (Architecture, building tools and services, speedy services and efficiency products)
PEACH	CHARITABLE IMAGING (Services and products for children, schools products, welfare organizations or charities)
YELLOW	COMMUNICATION (Yellow Pages, all services and products of the communication and entertainment industries, especially sales)
BRIGHT GREENS	INNOVATIVE IMAGING (Self-enhancement services and products, weight and diet centers, self-help services)
ALL GREENS	HEALTH, VEGETABLE, OR PLANT INDUSTRIES (Health food stores, homey restaurants, floral products and services)
LIGHT BLUE	CREATIVE IMAGES (Design or art industry, creative products or problem-solving services, computer products and servicing)

DARK BLUE	**EXECUTIVE IMAGING** (Business, education, and executive products and servicing
MAUVE OR PURPLE	**SPIRITUAL OR INTUITIVE IMAGING** (Training or services for emotional support. Sensitive imaging to the needs)
BROWN	**SUPPORT PRODUCTS AND SERVICES** (Businesses offering security, basic-needs and survival products)
BLACK	**AUTHORITY IMAGING** (Security or protection services. Sedate, severe, and aloof imaging)
WHITE	**INDIVIDUALISTIC OR SANITARY IMAGING** (Better with products than services as it will give an image of "aloneness")
GRAY	**PASSIVE OR EARTH-SUPPORT IMAGES** (Home repair services and products; stone and earth products, but not to image any services relating to human resources)
SILVER	**AN HONORABLE AND WORTHY IMAGE** (Legal services, money lending, and civil rights organizations)
GOLD	**IMAGES OF SECURITY AND WEALTH** (Brokers, bankers, merchants, and high-quality services)

7

Color Energy, a Natural Support

(Color guides for moods, attitudes, and feelings of well-being)

Have you ever begun the day feeling as if you've gotten up "on the wrong side of the bed"? Nothing felt quite right. You needed a "pick-me-up" color to wear for the day. The vibrational energy of color serves to change your mood as much as you will accept its service. Colors may even make you feel better about being alive, because they interact with you to perform whatever function is necessary. From depression, despair, or the blahs, colors can alter your attitude for the better. If colors are known to raise blood pressure (the reds), and calm overactive emotions (the greens), you can choose a color that will answer your energy need for each day.

Wearing the right colors can aid, encourage, strengthen, and support you. As you've already discovered, some inspire, ensure, protect, and also can act efficiently as attitude-change tools. All serve you as good performance supports and ego boosters. Look at the following chart to find what color can help you solve an attitude or mood problem for an extra boost each day.

In your wardrobe, use the color as an accent, such as in a scarf, tie, or belt. If you want a larger amount of color energy, try a mix-and-match coordinate such as a blouse or shirt, but don't wear it alone without a helper color. All tints and shades of each hue work well as your attitude changer or "pick-me-up" support.

COLOR	Feeling or Attitude to Change:
RED	Lack of physical energy Lack of strength or courage Feelings of unwantedness or rejection Negative thinking
PINK	Lack of self-acceptance Inability to love or nurture others Insensitivity to your own needs Emotional traumas
MAROON	Not enough love of life Intolerance of others Fear of being ugly and unloved Emotional insecurities concerning involvements
ORANGE	Lack of vitality Lack of motivation Uncertainty as to personal direction Inability to achieve results
PEACH	Lack of energy Inability to stabilize your emotions Insensitivity to the needs of others Low blood sugar levels
YELLOW	Despair or depression Loneliness or feelings of being alone Lack of open communication Feelings of frustration or limitations

MINT GREEN   Uncontrolled anger
Feelings of resentfulness
Lack of emotional control
Lack of patience

APPLE GREEN   Lack of new opportunities
Overdependency on others
Severe emotional stresses
Feeling overwhelmed by burdens of others

GREEN   Emotional confusion
Lack of clear insight and understanding
Feelings of anger
Lack of emotional stability

BLUE-GREEN   Lack of hope
(teal)   Lack of faith
Feelings of bewilderment
Need for more optimism

LIGHT BLUE   Mental dullness
Inability to see clearly
Lack of practicality
Indecisiveness

DARK BLUE   Fear of the unknown
Identity crisis
Inability to accept a leadership position
Nervousness and fear of traveling

MAUVE   Feeling fatigued from talking
Need for emotional relaxation
Lack of intuitive awareness
Minimizing phobias

PURPLE   Feelings of inferiority
Lack of inner peace
Guilt feelings
Excessive worry about imaginary problems

BROWN	Emotional insecurity Lack of physical stamina Uncertainties about future Fear of survival
BLACK	Need for extra emotional protection Supersensitivity to the environment Overresponsiveness to emotional stresses Fear of being taken advantage of
WHITE	Excessive worry or mental confusion Need for extra spiritual protection Fear of bad-habit addiction Need for more time and freedom
GRAY	Overwhelming feelings of stress Fear of invasion of privacy Emotional overinvolvements Mental fatigue
SILVER	Distrust of others Poor self-image Decreased self-worth Feelings of not performing satisfactorily
GOLD	Feelings of continuous victimization Lack of better goal opportunities Fear of accomplishment of success Insecurity concerning material gain

I have received many wonderful letters attesting to the power of color as an agent for attitude change, and how color has worked to aid people coping with the stresses of life. I would like to share a few of these with you.

(Letter 1—from a municipal employee, a social worker)

Dear Dottee,

I wanted to let you know how much I appreciate your support and insight and how helpful the SICA and my attitude support colors were for me last month, during the difficult time after my husband's death. I am feeling better and I have come to feel very grateful for the color, yellow, that you suggested I wear when depressed.

Each time when I found myself dwelling on the past and feeling sorry for myself, I put on my yellow blouse or sweater. I felt better and am grateful for the knowledge of how color can help one to cope. My husband also used his colors when he needed to shrug off heartache or loneliness. I like to think that they were helpful to him during his last days of life.

(Letter 2—from a high school principal)

Dear Dottee:

With your consultation, our high school has started to come alive with beautiful colors that are inspiring pride and creativity in our staff and students. During the years numerous classrooms and offices have been painted voluntarily by students, teachers, and office personnel. Our custodians are also voluntarily doing the graphic work in our hallways, and their excellent work has received much notice and praise.

As principal of the school, I have received accolades that I want to share with you. Many positive responses regarding the improved appearance and attitude of the students continually come from parents, staff members, and visitors to our school.

My gratitude goes to you for your expert assistance. Henry J. Kaiser once said, "When your work speaks for itself, don't interrupt." As I walk these halls, your work (colors) speaks. Many thanks.

(Letter 3—from a personnel administrator of a large factory)

Dear Dottee:

It was fun to evaluate and coordinate my wardrobe to help me present myself in my best colors. They have indeed helped my attitude. Here at work I've noticed that my colleagues are "sprucing up," not only the ladies but the men too. I'm sure that my SICA has rubbed off on them. Because I now understand "my" particular colors, I wear my clothes with new assurance.

I've also gained more inner awareness. The SICA gave me many insights regarding not only myself, but also into other people as well. The wearing of the right color at the right time has aided my attitude immensely.

Thank you again for a most rewarding experience. Hopefully, depending on next year's budget, other employees will be taking your SICA in the future.

(Letter 4—from a church program director)

Dear Dottee:

Our church has a new color scheme, new stained-glass windows, and a new attitude thanks to your work in selecting colors for the sanctuary and other areas of the church building. It's hard to believe that just a year ago our building had the same "ordinary" colors found in most churches. However, as soon as the sanctuary was painted in colors that you suggested, the minister and congregation decided that it was time to create a new set of stained-glass windows.

Within three months an artist had been commissioned to design a unique set of windows depicting the major religions of the world, the stained glass had been installed, and most importantly, the congregation had raised the entire $13,000 cost of the windows. During this time the church also redecorated the fellowship hall, remodeled the entrance area, painted the entire outside of the building, and generally gave the place the "face-lift" that was needed.

In additon to the new colors and new paint, there is a feeling of commitment and community that did not exist last year, which I attribute to the changes in the physical surroundings. This is now a church that people are proud of and excited about. I feel that your initial assistance with colors set us on the right track as we fulfill our spiritual purpose.

These letters attest to the helpful support that color has given to many in various professional fields. Color acted as an agent of support and change to the routine stresses of life. Whether it was placed on a wall or used as a natural support in the wardrobe, the result was the same—a knowledgeable use of color answered the need.

8

Color and Its Association With the Healing Arts

The history of color is interlaced with early pioneers in healing and science. From ancient Egypt and the isles of Greece to the Italian peninsula and the city of Rome, color was spoken as one of the languages for health. Pythagoras, Hermes, Hippocrates, Democritus, Aristotle, and Galen, just to mention a few, all gave credibility to color as an "outward expression" of an internal pathological condition. Although centuries apart, the physicians Pythagoras in Greece and Galen in Rome treated with colors. Pythagoras was reported to have used color and music to cure disease, while Galen believed that external application of color could encourage the healing of an internal condition. Hippocrates, the renowned physician who wrote the oath that all medical doctors follow today, found that the color of a patient's skin determined the condition of their health. His theory was that a flushed or reddened skin indicated circulatory disease, a yellow appearance gave the sign of stomach or liver involvement, and blue to black discoloration of the body showed a terminal illness. He prescribed many treatments and medicines based on his diagnostic attitude toward skin discoloration.

But if I could retravel the avenues of time, the physician that I would enjoy meeting today would be the eleventh-century Persian Islamic philosopher and healer Avicenna—the father of color therapy. Far, far from Rome and Greece, this passionate man influenced all of Europe. Not only did he use color for diagnosis, but also as a cure. In his *Canon of Medicine* he gave credit to color as a most important curative; he even wrapped his patients in red bandages to stimulate their circulation for healing. Avicenna was known throughout Europe for his red cloak, which he wore as a physician's mantle. In a later era, English physicians copied his attire, but sadly not his example of healing. Hundreds of years passed before color therapy again became recognized as a treatment for illness.

Color healing surfaced again in late nineteenth-century America due to the efforts of Edwin D. Babbitt, a mystic, artist, and physician. Like Avicenna, Dr. Babbit expounded upon the relationship between color and medicine. In his journal, *The Principles of Light and Color*, published in 1878, he chose the three primaries—red, yellow, and blue—as the basic healing rays of color. He felt that each color had an opposite color that affected the return of balance to the body. For example, if a person was reacting overemotionally (red), he would expose them to a treatment of green light, which would calm their emotions and bring them back to balance. Although much of his research was discounted by the medical profession, his theories are being reexamined today and their intrinsic value is being recognized.

This chapter will deal specifically with the wearing of colors as personal resources to aid health. Art therapies have attempted to explore and explain the emotional significance of color and form. Not much information is available on the wearing of colors to aid certain problems. Some therapists feel that the excessive use of black in the wardrobe indicates negative qualities, but as yet this too has not been scientifically proven. Black, however, isn't all bad, for it might be used as a positive color if one is wearing it to protect a sensitive nature.

Creatively, you, as your own self-healer, can use the electromagnetic energy of color to give you added support to help you on your way back to health. We, as human beings, emanate energy fields, discovered and named "corona discharges" in 1939 by the Soviet photographer-scientist Semyon Kirlian. The world revealed by these "radiation field photographs" showed that plant leaves, coins, jewelry, and human appendages were all surrounded by "halos" of energy. Invisible to the human eye, vibrations of energy swirl around and out from us, like "reaching out" hands or antennas. Recognize the love feelings or electric energy that you receive from another, or the magnetism of a famous personality filling a room with their presence; all exemplify this movement of energy.

Many great European painters of the past, such as the early Italian art masters Fra Angelico and Giotto, along with other well-known "halo" artists, have attempted to portray these human rainbows. None painted them the same, not in shape, size, or form, but all visualized them as extensions of the human body. For those of you who are into the New Age philosophies, you already comprehend that we have an energy body as well as a physical one. Both react to all outside stimulants. Those early sensitive artists did indeed paint the auras, and futurists for tomorrow project that science will be exploring them for clues to health. This chapter will help you to understand how your energy fields respond to color.

Colors react and interact with your vibrations to balance, weaken, or support. When you hurt or want a natural Band-Aid for relief, the energy of a color might just be the thing to help.

Following is a chart to guide you in the use of color application or the wearing of colors for natural healing support. Not all this information is, as yet, documented by science and research. Yet, around the country, many researchers into natural therapies are trying colors for healing. Without waiting for scientific approval, these practitioners of the healing arts are using colors for their soothing and beneficial effects. "Color support has improved countless clients' health and resistance to stress,

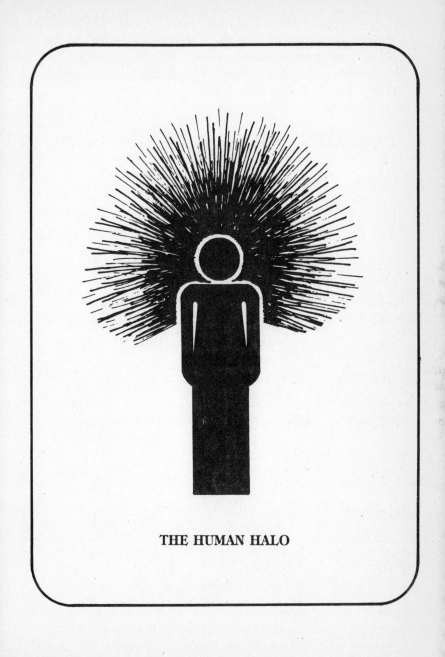

THE HUMAN HALO

combined with balanced nutrition and exercises," writes Michelle Lusson in her book, *Creative Wellness, a Holistic Guide to Total Health.* These and other statements are gradually increasing the public's awareness that color does help.

COLORS FOR HEALTH SUPPORT

COLOR	Good for:	Not Good For:
RED	Upper or lower backache Colds and flus All sprains and muscle disorders Healing of burns	Coronary diseases (May use blue-greens)
PINK	Heart spasms or angina Circulatory problems Blood disorders Asthmas	Weight problems (May use dark blue)
MAROON	Female disorders (such as cramps) Stiff necks Complexion problems Aching or cold feet	Thyroid dysfunctions (May use peach)
ORANGE	Arthritis or joint stiffness Constipation Stiff joints Lower-back aches	Hyperactivity Alcoholism (May use light blues)
PEACH	Dieting Lower-bowel problems Digestive disorders	Headaches (May use light purples)

YELLOW	Adrenal weakness Bladder or kidney Mental depression Food allergies	Drug addiciton or liver/gall bladder disorders (May use browns)
MINT GREEN	Fevers Stomachaches Infections Sinus problems	Adrenal weakness or stress prevention (May use maroon)
GREEN	High blood pressure Colitis or diarrhea Eye problems Weight problems	Allergies (May use golds or deep yellows)
LIGHT BLUE	Sunburn Fluid retention problems Sore throats Hyperactivity	Insomnia or sleeping problems Mental stress (May use deep pinks)
DARK BLUE	Leg spasms Thyroid disorders Impaired smell or taste Physical coordination problems	Lung problems (May use pale yellows)
PURPLE	Headaches Addictions Sleep problems Sexual overstimulation	Female disorders especially cramps (May use reds)
BROWN	Weight loss Hypoglycemia or diabetes Female hormone imbalance Bone structure weakness	Lower-bowel problems (May use peach)

COLOR	Good for:	Not Good For:
BLACK	Muscular weakness Overactive glandular function Nervousness (excessive)	Depression or moodiness (May use yellows)
GRAY	Muscular tensions Stress-related illnesses Poor digestion and bloating Inflammation and swelling	Lower-back aches (May use maroon)
WHITE	Itching Dermatitis or heat rash Muscular spasms	Digestive disorders (May use peach or blue-greens)

9

Share the Language of Color

As new methods of satellite communication bridge the continents of the world, color and its emanations are becoming a medium of universal exchange. SICA is the lexicon or grammar of the language of color, a new form of nonverbal communication. Some of you have already discovered your personal sensitivity to the hues of the rainbow, while others, desiring to know more about themselves, are still testing their inner feelings for colors. SICA is one of those new forms of nonverbal communications. For those of you who like self-analyzing methods, SICA is now for you an uncomplicated tool for self-portrait visualization. It will always be easy to administer as it is fun, as straightforward as saying hello—no more complex than a child's coloring book.

The art students who helped design it discovered that SICA motivated and inspired them to reach out for new horizons and the fulfillment of their dreams. For its color message alone, many people have utilized their SICA self-portrait to improve their personal and professional relationships. It can also be used as a personal image and design counselor for getting the most power out of yourself. When you're at odds with yourself, or you just need that extra boost, your colors can return you to balance naturally.

I hope that with the book you have found a new method to heighten your awareness of your talents through the language of color, and the use of your personal colors. It has also been my intent to show how color itself, a natural energy, can give you support—even physical support—better communications, and most important, a new intuitive insight into yourself. Share it with another!

Bibliography

Babbit, Edwin D. *The Principles of Light and Color.* Published originally in 1878, East Orange, NJ: by the author. Currently reprinted by Citadel Press, Secaucus, NJ.

Birren, Faber. *Color, a Survey in Words and Pictures, From Ancient Mysticism to Modern Science.* Secaucus, NJ: University Books, 1963.

Gruner, O. Cameron. *A Treatise on the Canon of Medicine of Avicenna.* London: Luzac & Co., 1930.

Jackson, Carole. *Color Me Beautiful.* New York: Ballantine Books, 1981.

Kandinsky, Wassily. *The Art of Spiritual Harmony.* Boston: Houghton Mifflin Co., 1914.

Luscher, Dr. Max. *The Luscher Color Test.* New York: Pocket Books, 1969.

Lusson, Michelle. *Creative Wellness, a Holistic Guide to Total Health.* New York: Warner Books, 1987.

The Rainbow Book. Edited by F. Lanier Graham. New York: Vintage Books, a division of Random House, NY, 1979.

The writings and philosophies of these pioneers in the field of color and color research inspired me in my work to synthesize my theories into practical applications, but most important, to remain true to my beliefs—**color is a universal language.**

For further information, write

Domel Color Communications
P.O. Box 3829
Albuquerque, NM 87110